WANG JIANLIN

&

DALIAN WANDA

Published by
LID Publishing Limited
The Record Hall, Studio 204, 16-16a Baldwins Gardens,
London EC1N 7RJ, United Kingdom

31 West 34th Street, 8th Floor, Suite 8004,
New York, NY 10001, US

info@lidpublishing.com
www.lidpublishing.com

A member of:

www.businesspublishersroundtable.com

Published in collaboration with the China Translation & Publishing House
(a member of the China Publishing Group Corporation)

 China Translation and Publishing House

© LID Publishing Limited, 2017
© China Translation and Publishing House, 2017

Printed in Great Britain by TJ International
ISBN: 978-1-911498-27-8

Illustration: Myriam El Jerari
Cover and Page design: Caroline Li

WANG JIANLIN

& DALIAN WANDA

BY **ZHOU XUAN**

LONDON   MONTERREY
MADRID   SHANGHAI
MEXICO CITY   BOGOTA
NEW YORK   BUENOS AIRES
BARCELONA   SAN FRANCISCO

PREFACE

China has Wanda and Wanda has Wang Jianlin. Wang Jianlin joined the army in 1970. In 1986 he transferred to a civilian job and became the office director of the local People's Government in Xigang district, Dalian city. In 1989 he became the managing director of Dalian Wanda Group Co. Ltd. He has remained in that position to this day. The *Hurun Report* – a magazine which ranks China's wealthiest individuals – stated in October 2015 that Wang Jianlin's assets had reached the value of ¥220 billion, making him once more the richest man in China.

During the rapid development of China's economy over the course of the past 30 years, there has been no shortage of tales of wealth of every kind. The protagonists have been just as manifold. Yet the tide ebbs and flows and it has been rare to see one linger at the top for long. How has Wang Jianlin managed to climb, slowly but steadily, all the way to the very top to be crowned China's richest man?

Wang Jianlin was born into a Red family. His father was a Red Army veteran from the War of Resistance against Japan (1937–1945). That is why the army and soldiers have always had a special place in Wang Jianlin's heart. When he was 15 years old, he resolutely left home to enlist in the army in Jilin province. At that time, he was the youngest recruit in his regiment, yet he never asked for special treatment on account of his youth. His courageous, enduring spirit earned him new-found admiration from his comrades-in-arms.

Wang Jianlin developed a fearless, unyielding nature while in the army. It was also at this time that he started his quest for self-enrichment through knowledge. He used what spare time he had to expand his knowledge in a number of different fields. As time went by, Wang Jianlin did not rest content with his comfortable post in the army. Instead, as the wave of reform and opening-up swept through the country, he made a single-minded decision to take off his military uniform and make the transition to a civilian job. It was then that the tale of Wanda Group started in earnest.

For 30 years, Wang Jianlin has been forging the way for Wanda Group. He has guided it from the housing development sector, commercial real estate and the football industry through to the film, television, theatre and internet industries. The former private soldier Wang Jianlin has become a commercial magnate worth hundreds of billions. As for Wanda, it turned from a tiny debt-ridden company on the verge of bankruptcy into the world-renowned, successful multinational corporation that it is today.

As for Wanda's future development and direction, we can only wait and see. I believe that under Wang Jianlin's persevering leadership, guided by stability and innovation, Wanda's awesome flight will surely continue to command the world's attention.

CONTENTS

CHAPTER ONE
A HIGH-SPIRITED YOUTH   9

CHAPTER TWO
A REAL ESTATE EMPIRE   31

CHAPTER THREE
DESTINED FOR FOOTBALL   59

CHAPTER FOUR
BUILDING A FOUNDATION FOR THE WORLD   81

CHAPTER FIVE
A THOUGHT OF A CENTURY LASTS FOR A CENTURY   97

APPENDICES
TRANSCRIPTS OF TWO RECENT PUBLIC SPEECHES
BY WANG JIANLIN

APPENDIX 1
REPORT ON THE WORK OF WANDA GROUP IN 2015
(16 JANUARY 2016, XISHUANGBANNA)   130

APPENDIX 2
GOING GLOBAL – THE WANDA WAY
(23 FEBRUARY 2016, OXFORD UNIVERSITY)   166

CHAPTER 1

A HIGH-SPIRITED YOUTH

A RED FAMILY

Wang Jianlin's father, Wang Yiquan, was a Red Army soldier from a peasant family. He took part in the Long March (1934–1935) and the War of Resistance (1937–1945). However, there is little consensus about his status once he retired from the army. Rumours have it that he was the deputy head of the organizational department of the Sichuan Party committee, or that he took on the role of deputy chairman of the Tibet Autonomous Region. Wang Jianlin has neither confirmed nor rejected these rumours, and his resolute silence has, however unintentionally, contributed to their growth. The expansion and development of his Wanda Empire has always been accompanied by public speculation regarding his family.

In fact, Wang Yiquan was nowhere near as important as many people assumed. He had only ever worked at the forestry commission at the county level. He was the deputy director general for Dakin county (later renamed Jinchuan county) Forestry Commission.

Although, in reality, Wang Yiquan did not hold such a high position as was rumoured, he gave himself the title of 'little red soldier'. He was lucky enough to be part of the Northern Expedition in 1930 and to return back home with the glorious victory in 1949. Among the other 'little red soldiers', however, he did not hold an especially high position.

From 1958 onwards, Wang Yiquan enjoyed a good reputation in the Dakin county Forestry Commission. His prestige far outreached that of the director general or the secretary. He did not have the airs of an official and was well respected by his colleagues. Many also envied his ¥80 monthly salary. Starting from 1956, the whole country had undergone a wage reform. Natural conditions, price of commodities, quality of life and the wage situation were all factored in. At that time the country was divided into 11 regions with different salary scales. Going up each level was equal to a salary rise of ¥2. Dakin county belonged to the ninth level, so the wage base was high. Local graduates with a bachelor's degree could expect to earn ¥60. In the whole county, the people with the highest salaries were the county Party chairman, the political commissar on military matters, and after that came Wang Yiquan.

The Wang family always had enough food to eat, which was considered very lucky at that time. Wang Yiquan even had enough spare money and time to care for some poor children from the countryside. Li Hongyou and his friends, still students at the time, often enjoyed ice lollies and sweets bought by Wang Yiquan. Li Hongyou described Wang Yiquan as being a friendly, bubbly, great "old chap" who liked a laugh.

Jinchuanese people like to chat and spend their free time gossiping. Wang Yiquan liked to tell the children of the other staff about his experiences of fighting the Japanese. He would invite them over for tea, gathering a large audience on the way. He would then describe to them in every little detail how to assemble a gun or a bayonet. Almost everyone in Dakin county knew that Wang Jianlin's dad was a Red Army veteran who had fought the Japanese.

Wang Yiquan held a firm belief in communism. He liked to tell the students about the importance of love for the motherland and love of the Party. He also liked to instruct them on how best to build up the nation for the future. Li Hongyou and his friends considered Wang Yiquan's ideas outdated.

Wang Yiquan's approach also influenced the way he brought up his sons. He had always been very strict. He stressed over and over again the importance of striving hard, studying well, reading more when given the chance and becoming a Party cadre. In keeping with his history as a military cadre, he was always blunt and direct.

His father's prestige made the young Wang Jianlin feel proud. During that fervent era, Red Army veterans were worshipped and looked up to. Living in his father's shadow, Wang Jianlin also enjoyed a certain level of adoration from his peers.

On New Year's Day 1953, Wang Yiquan got married. The matchmaker was a district committee secretary. His wife-to-be was called Qin Jialan. She was 18 years younger than Wang Yiquan. Qin Jialan was very satisfied with her arranged marriage. She often used to say that Wang Yiquan had always made her feel as though she was the boss in their marriage. He never bullied her into anything.

In the 1950s the family moved to the county city of Da-kin in the Aba prefecture. This was a good thing according to Qin Jialan: "People were dying of hunger everywhere, but we were lucky enough to have a rabbit each week." There were many barren mountains in the county that no one tended to. Qin Jialan used to cross the steel chain bridge into the mountains by herself to cultivate barren land and improve the family's livelihood. She did not shy away from growing vegetables and raising rabbits. Later on, when she recalled a large Russian beetroot with leaves growing on top, Qin Jialan, then in her eighties, seemed especially content. A beetroot weighing a kilo or a kilo and a half was enough to satisfy the needs of the whole family. "Peel the skin, cut the beetroot into thin slices and fry it. The children can feast on the dried beetroot slices; they love them. The leaves can then be given to the rabbits."

Wang Jianlin spent his childhood years with a remote, resource-rich highland plateau on his doorstep. Given his father's special treatment at work and his mother's industriousness, Wang Jianlin lived an unusually comfortable life. In his childhood years, he was not only the oldest son at home but also the 'gang leader' among his friends. Such status gave him the first chance to practise the management skills that he would develop later in life. He proved to be a charismatic leader, be it at the head of a gang of ten kids or as the manager of a company with over 100,000 employees.

No one knows whether Wang Jianlin as a child already strove to carve out a piece of the pie for himself, or whether the young man Wang Jianlin already harboured ambition in his heart. But at least one thing is certain – he was far removed from the commercialized world. He grew up in a calm and leisurely little town with his family, away from the hubbub of large cities.

While working at the forestry commission, his father, Wang Yiquan, was in charge of salary distribution. He controlled the payroll system and distributed office supplies. Qin Jialan took care of the day-to-day running of the household. In the evenings she went out to cultivate the barren land. Wang Jianlin was the eldest son in the family, and it was not long before he became his father's primary helping hand. The hard work he had to shoulder blurred the boundary between his childhood and youth years. Like so many others of his generation, Wang Jianlin had to take on the burden of responsibility for his family at a young age. As a result, he became more mature and had soon gained more experience than would be expected at his age.

Qin Jialan liked to say over and over again that Wang Jianlin was the eldest son in the family. He had four younger brothers who all did as he said. According to tradition, the eldest son took on the role of the father, which made his burden even heavier. Wang Yiquan's five sons had always been the main working force in the family. Wang Jianlin, being the eldest, always worked in the fields with the greatest vigour. Qin Jialan rested easy knowing that her eldest son was a good role model for his brothers. He also took on the task of checking his brothers' homework for them.

In her old age Qin Jialan could not recall clearly the details of past events, but she never forgot to emphasize that it was mainly thanks to Wang Jianlin that the family could live such a comfortable life. Wang Jianlin once jokingly asked his mother: "Who made you give birth to so many brothers for me?"

Before Wang Jianlin reached adolescence, he had firmly established his role as the eldest in the family. This long-term leadership status also made him the natural leader of his childhood playmates.

The youthful Wang Jianlin could think for himself. He was naughty and independent. When the boys got into a fight, he loved to take the lead.

The backyard of the forestry commission was spacious and well suited for the mock fighting and chasing games of boys who had too much energy. As with many other boys who grew up in poverty, the games that Wang Jianlin played were cheap ones like hide and seek, climbing trees or firing slingshots. Wang Jianlin took the lead to make everyone play with just as much enthusiasm, regardless of whether they were his peers or younger brothers.

And, like many other children of forestry commission employees, when Wang Jianlin was old enough to go to school he went to the Dongfanghong Primary School in Dakin county. Dongfanghong Primary School was one of the best schools in the Aba prefecture, known for rigorous discipline. Apart from the two main subjects – mathematics and Chinese – the students also studied the arts, music, physical education and other subjects. The extracurricular activities were plentiful as well, from drawing classes to camping in the wilderness and climbing mountains. In busy seasons the students lent a hand at cultivating the land and helped peasants harvest wheat, which took up most of their free time.

During his primary school years, Wang Jianlin was no different from other students, apart from the fact that he was the class representative. He liked to play basketball, even though later on in life he was to have a much closer and longer-lasting relationship with another sport – football. Occasionally he excelled at attacking during matches, but on the whole he was just a novice without any extraordinary talent.

After graduating from primary school he enrolled in the only local secondary school – Dakin Secondary School. Judged by the quality of teaching, it was the top secondary school in the area. Almost one fifth of the teachers were university or college graduates.

Wang Jianlin studied at Dakin for seven years. At that time the forestry commission just happened to be recruiting the children of its employees into the forest management bureau. At this point, Wang Jianlin left school to become a member of the logging team. The majority of the city kids were unwilling to stoop so low. Most of the enlisted workers came from the countryside, but Wang Jianlin was one of the toughest.

Wang Jianlin was assigned to the logging team based at Maerzu town. The day-to-day life of loggers was very regular. They got up at 7am. At 7.30am they attended a safety briefing. They started work at 8am and finished at 5pm. Their journey from home to their place of work included an hour's walk along a mountain path. During his days at Maerzu, Wang Jianlin lived in a brick house that belonged to the forestry station. Maerzu was tucked far away in a mountain valley, almost ten kilometres from Dakin. To get from the headquarters to Maerzu, one first had to walk four to five kilometres along the road to the mouth of the valley and then climb another three or four kilometres to the forestry station, which took about four hours. If Wang Jianlin was lucky, he could catch a ride from a passing car; if not, then he could only rely on his legs to get him there. He earned ¥30-40 each month for working at the forestry station.

Wang Jianlin's main job was to fell trees. As jobs in the logging industry go, this was considered to be a relatively easy one. Every day he had to cut down 100 small trees. Once he was finished he could return home.

Apart from felling trees, however, Wang Jianlin had another job to do – burning charcoal. He had to cut the trunk into small logs which he would then place inside a kiln. Once it was burned, he would take out the charcoal and seal the kiln. After a day of charcoal burning, he was black from head to toe. He then went from house to house handing out the charcoal to the staff.

At the age of 15 or 16, Wang Jianlin was very different in the eyes of his colleagues from other children his age. Every day, he had to walk up a mountain for one hour to get to work. This lasted for almost a year. No one knows what was going through Wang Jianlin's head when he was working at the forestry station.

In 1969, as Wang Jianlin was moving from school to adult society, the Zhenbao Island conflict broke out. This emergency military situation forced China to increase its military forces. At this point Wang Jianlin, who had been working at the forestry station for just over a year, decided to join the army. It was at this point that he embarked on a new stage in his life.

NEW RECRUIT

According to Wanda Corporation official documents, Wang Jianlin joined the army in 1969. He officially enlisted in the army and joined the Shengyang garrison in December 1969, but according to military records he could only count as a soldier from 1970 on. Wang Jianlin harboured a fervent passion to serve his country. His enthusiasm was admirable, yet he trod an uneasy path in the military. The Aba prefecture is an ethnic minority region. Youths with permanent residence in the city that relied on commodity grain were not allowed to join the army. In order for Wang Jianlin to be accepted, Qin Jialan first had to send him to her home in Cangxi where he could gain first-hand experience of living in the countryside and only then could he join up.

When Wang Jianlin first mentioned his intention of joining the army, he had Qin Jialan's full support. She thought that the young generation should inherit and carry on glorious old traditions. It made sense for her eldest son to be a soldier. There were nine other children of employees who joined the forestry industry bureau along with Wang Jianlin. Among the nine, Wang Jianlin did not perform any better than anyone else. It is almost impossible to link his old acquaintances' impressions of him with the billionaire who now sits atop the Chinese commercial world. Some of his old acquaintances even say that if he had not joined the army he would have spent his entire life in Dakin county. At most, he might have become a middle-ranking official. He would most likely not have achieved even as much as his father had.

After Wang Jianlin left Dakin, he stayed in the countryside in his home town of Cangxi. Not long after, he joined the army and was posted to Jilin province. He once revealed in an interview that when he was leaving his home town, his mother told him: "Do your best to be a good soldier. Strive to do better than your father." Wang Jianlin took his mother's repeated exhortation to heart. In the same year that he joined the army, he lived up to his mother's expectations and had already become the 'good soldier' that she had urged him to be.

While in the army, Wang Jianlin kept up his habit of writing letters to Qin Jialan. At first he wrote two letters a month. Gradually the frequency of his letters declined, but he kept the habit up all the time until he went to Dalian. Altogether, Qin Jialan stored over 300 letters in a chest where she collected her son's impressions from his time in the army.

A comrade-in-arms later posted on Weibo, the popular Chinese microblogging site, his recollections of Wang Jianlin's conduct during his first time in an unfamiliar environment: "At the start of spring 1971, a group of new recruits arrived at the army camp that was nestled in the middle of the mountains on the bank of the Yalu River in Jian county, Jilin province. This was the first time I saw Wang Jianlin. They were members of a special reconnaissance squad. Among the new recruits were boys from Sichuan province and from Fushun county in Liaoning province. The squadron head started picking soldiers from the new recruits to join the reconnaissance squad. He first chose two soldiers from Fushun and then he walked over to a thin soldier of small stature and asked him whether or not he wanted to be a scout. The soldier agreed." That soldier was Wang Jianlin.

The youthful Wang Jianlin was nowhere near as tall and well-built as he is today. The army uniform was too big for him, the leather hat was too large and the boots did not fit properly. Couple that with his slight stature and he looked very comical indeed. But despite his less than glamorous outer appearance, Wang Jianlin knew that opportunities were hard to come by and had no intention of missing out. During his career as a scout in the reconnaissance squad for the Shenyang military region, he learned to take advantage of every opportunity and he trained himself to face up to every challenge.

As a regular scout, besides the usual outdoor military training, Wang Jianlin was also trained to overcome obstacles, break into an enemy camp, steal classified documents and draw encoded sketches. These were the basic skills required of a scout. Apart from these tasks, if there was a need, the scouts had to sneak into a cemetery in the dead of night and check one gravestone after another, just to see whether or not there was a slip of paper hidden there before the owner's death. All of this was meant to train their nerves and courage.

Although Wang Jianlin was a new recruit, he nonetheless prepared himself to be able to handle all sorts of unthinkable training exercises. In an interview with the media later on in life, he said that before he joined the army he specifically got a book on thanatology – the scientific and sociological study of death – to help prepare himself for all the possible eventualities that he might have to face in the future. This habit of his allowed him to thrive and grow as a person in the army. He continued to make one breakthrough after another. Decades later, when people from around the world came to scrutinize this boy who had joined the army at just 15 or 16 years old, they saw that he had learned to welcome change and uncertainty with open arms and that he was well adapted to swiftly make the right decision.

Wang Jianlin took to heart the importance the army placed on being organized. He endlessly strove to learn from it. Later on, when he was building his tremendous business empire, the guiding principles that were still imprinted on his brain came in very useful.

During his time in the army, the high-spirited and youthful Wang Jianlin had undergone a change from a muddleheaded boy to a military scout. To some extent this was the turning point in his life. Although he was never aware of it himself, it is a fact that cannot be denied. In his subsequent career in the commercial world he polished the skills he had learned in the army and reused them on the market – this was how he ensured his continual success in every field.

PLANNING, NOT MEDIOCRITY, IS THE KEY

At the time that Wang Jianlin joined the army, planned economy was still practised in China. It was considered good luck for an ordinary person to be able to join the army and in that way ensure they would have enough to eat. What more could one want? Although, in comparison with ordinary civilians, soldiers led relatively well-off lives, life in the army provided little in the way of leisure activities. Getting together for a chat or singing war songs were the only forms of group entertainment. Apart from these, there was hardly any other way for soldiers to pass their free time. On the other hand, thanks to the monotony of army life, Wang Jianlin and his comrades-in-arms had the opportunity to expand their knowledge and learn new skills. They did not waste their time on entertainment.

Wang Jianlin laid out a plan for his life: to study. Today we have countless devices to help us study, but Wang Jianlin's studying at the time consisted simply of reading books. Later on, Wang Jianlin, together with some of his comrades-in-arms, decided to enrol in a long-distance correspondence course at Liaoning University. The university was not far away, but soldiers were not allowed to attend; they were not even given the opportunity to sit in on a single lecture.

And so, in those days, apart from the daily compulsory training and other jobs, Wang Jianlin and his comrades-in-arms spent most of their free time studying. They made use of every spare minute and second they had to satisfy their thirst for knowledge.

Faced with unfavourable, or even harsh circumstances, Wang Jianlin fully devoted himself to studying. In this way he was able to push away the loneliness associated with monotonous army life. Indeed, studying made him feel that he was living a rich life. He was not alone in feeling this way, as many other soldiers were of the same mind.

For the most part, Wang Jianlin and his friends were typical hot-blooded youths bursting with energy. The reason they chose to join the army was that they harboured youthful passions. They wanted to make the army their career. That is also what gave them the motivation to study. They all shared a thirst for knowledge. In order to increase the efficacy of their studies, they spontaneously formed a study group. Whenever they came across a difficult question, they all gathered together to talk it through.

In 1974, Wang Jianlin completed all of the self-study courses at Liaoning University and received a diploma. It was in that year that he joined the Chinese Communist Party. He was naturally excited and delighted by these achievements, but he did not become complacent as he knew that his achievements only proved that he had made the first step towards reaching his dream and realizing his self-value. They showed that hard work gets repaid with reward.

The period of self-study during his military career instilled the habit of studying from which Wang Jianlin has benefited throughout his life. It seemed that there was always a voice deep in his heart that called out a steady stream of encouragement to him. This voice revealed to him his shortcomings and constantly urged him to improve.

From the day that Wang Jianlin obtained his diploma from the long-distance correspondence course at Liaoning University, he showed no sign of being overly proud that his efforts had been rewarded. On the contrary, he strove to realize his dreams with even more urgency than before. During his four years of being tempered by the army, he had progressed from being a new recruit to a regular soldier.

Wang Jianlin's relentless hard work earned him constant approval from his superiors. Not long after, he got reassigned to assume the post of propaganda officer. He had no experience in this area, having joined the military straight after graduating from secondary school. His new position was in no way similar to his role in local government. Although he lacked experience, he did not back away from the challenge; instead, he threw himself into the work with the utmost zeal.

Whenever he came across an aspect of his work that he did not understand, he asked his comrades to teach him. Before long he got used to his new post in the propaganda department. Wang Jianlin approached every task with an attitude of perseverance. Because of this, he was often regarded as one of the best propaganda officers. On several occasions he received public praise from his superiors. Each year he received several letters of commendation from the military bureau. He was even awarded a certificate for an outstanding contribution to the work of the propaganda department.

People say that to succeed once may be a coincidence, but Wang Jianlin went from one success to the next. Surely this must have been down to his outstanding skill. For Wang Jianlin, this extraordinary skill could only be obtained through constant study. He has always believed, even after building his Wanda empire, that if a person did not study then he was doomed to a life of mediocrity.

In 1978, Dalian Military Academy in Liaoning province started enrolling new students. At the time the academy only accepted outstanding officers and soldiers from the

Shenyang region. In that year Wang Jianlin was recommended by his platoon leader to join the eighth subunit of squadron 2 in group 2, infantry unit 1 in the military academy. Wang Jianlin made a deep impression on both his comrades-in-arms and his teachers. The key words people used to describe him were 'hard-working', 'kind' and 'independent-thinking'.

In August 1980, two years after his enrolment, Wang Jianlin graduated from Dalian Military Academy with outstanding grades. He accepted the honour of staying on at the academy, assuming the post of staff officer. At that time a man with the talent of Wang Jianlin was hard to come by. There were several thousand officers undergoing training at the academy, but only two or three stayed on. He was one of those that stayed behind, which speaks for itself.

During his time as staff officer, Wang Jianlin made use of his literary talents – writing essays and composing poems. At times, when everyone gathered together for a chat in their free time, Wang Jianlin came prepared with a notebook and a pen. A few days after he would have a newspaper printed out ready, complete with news, articles and reviews. *Dalian Daily*, *People's Daily* and *Liberation Daily* became his inseparable companions. The Shenyang military region had a newspaper of its own at the time – *Forward Daily*. It almost served as a special column for Wang Jianlin.

Wang Jianlin's artistic talents were not limited to writing essays and composing poems. He also excelled at playing the *erhu* – a kind of Chinese fiddle. He was very fond of contemporary writers such as the poet Hai Zi, poet and novelist Gu Cheng, and the novelist and essayist Yi Shu; but he preferred to write realistically. Most of his works pertain to military life and army training. There is even a good number of war cries in his poems. Time and again, Wang Jianlin used his unconventional yet highly structured method of studying to reap the fruits of success.

DREAMING OF BECOMING A GENERAL

As time went by, Wang Jianlin's talents gradually unfolded in the army camp. Impressed by his literary gifts, his superiors applied for permission from the top level and transferred him to the Academy's propaganda department so as not to waste his talents. Wang Jianlin's main task at the time was to take charge of relations with external universities and help the soldiers that were enrolled at the military academy to pursue further study.

It was through relentless studying that Wang Jianlin not only turned from a new recruit in the eyes of his comrades to a regular soldier, but also became an official who earned the appreciation of his superiors. As his ability continued to grow, he was promoted to battalion secretary.

In 1982 Wang Jianlin was 28 years old. At this point he took the first steps on his journey to the top. The future held even greater potential for development. He did not become complacent with his achievements, though, and never paused from chasing after his dream. As the needs of the army required, his superiors arranged for Wang Jianlin to assume the role of chief of staff. The way that Wang Jianlin saw it, no matter what he was asked to do, as long as it was required in his job, he would think of a way of successfully completing his task. For two years he buried himself in his work.

During these two years he fumbled his way through his work and did his best to learn the required knowledge.

Gradually he increased his understanding of administrative and financial management. In this way he built a firm base for managing over 100,000 Wanda employees in the future. Wang Jianlin's frequent job transfers resulted in his unconsciously expanding his knowledge in a wide variety of fields.

In 1983, Wang Jianlin started attending a Party and government specialized training course at Liaoning University. Three years later he graduated with outstanding grades and obtained a degree in economic management. At that time, specialized training courses were similar to university courses today. They, too, were divided into subjects. The majority of soldiers chose subjects that were closely related to military management, so that they could readily put their knowledge into practice. Subjects like economics, industry and commerce, or literature were the least popular and hardly anyone applied for them.

In 1986, Wang Jianlin became deputy director of the management office at the military academy. He now ranked with deputy regimental commanders. It was indeed rare to see someone assume this post at such a young age. As the deputy director of the management office, he was responsible for the logistics of the entire academy. His work also included attending to relations with individual members of the public and with the government. The management post allowed him to interact more with the outside world. It was during this time that he honed his communication skills. He also came into contact with more senior people and dealt with ever more complicated problems.

Although Wang Jianlin was now in a position of power, he was modest and unassuming. He never offended anyone and always left a good impression on anyone he met.

Whenever a member of the public wished to contact the academy, he would do his utmost to make it possible. Perhaps it was at this time that he first harboured the thought of leaving the army.

As his skills multiplied, the dream of becoming a general that he held in his heart was ever more tangible. But, just as he started planning how to realize his dream and expand his opportunities to study and grow, he was unexpectedly faced with a decision that put him to the test. It all happened very quickly and Wang Jianlin had no time to prepare himself.

In 1985, the Central Military Committee, under the watchful eye of the whole world, made the decision to reduce the personnel of the People's Liberation Army by 1 million. Wang Jianlin was faced with a life-changing decision. What options were open to a soldier in such a large-scale disarmament? Transfer to a civilian job was a distinct possibility.

As soon as the disarmament order was given, turmoil broke out in Wang Jianlin's unit. Disarmament was different from ordinary retirement or transfer to civilian work, as the soldiers that were to retire or transfer were notified in advance and therefore had time to prepare themselves. This disarmament order, however, came all of a sudden. Furthermore, the order was to be carried out according to each region's individual circumstances, which meant that anyone could be selected for disarmament.

All of a sudden, the soldiers' mood plummeted, as in the near future, any one of them could be asked to lay aside their uniform. Wang Jianlin was no different. He had joined the army with a dream. Through unyielding effort, he had gradually made his dream more and more real, but just as he was bracing himself to take the final step to the peak, it was as if he had suddenly lost his footing and plummeted back down to earth.

Wang Jianlin asked himself: If I really were to shed my military uniform, what else could I do? Such a dilemma had no easy solution for a boy who had joined the army at just 15 or 16 years of age. But he soon came up with an answer – hadn't his father himself also transferred to a civilian job? And wasn't he just as good in his new post?

Wang Jianlin thought long and hard about the disarmament problem. Unlike most people, he dug deeper to find an answer. He wanted to understand the real reason behind the disarmament order. He knew that the government first and foremost strove to develop the country's economy, but lacked the strength to do so. From the government's point of view, the military department naturally was the heaviest burden on the country's expenses. The army was a guarantee of national stability, but in peacetime the nation needed to aim for quality rather than quantity. At the moment, the country spent the majority of its expenses on the military, which naturally meant that it lacked the resources to stimulate the development of the regional economy. Moreover, if the nation was unable to become prosperous and strong, then all of the nation's citizens had no way of realizing their own small ambitions.

Once Wang Jianlin had thoroughly thought everything through, he resolutely came up with a surprising decision: answering the call for disarmament, he applied to be transferred to a civilian job.

It takes quite some courage for an experienced soldier to make the decision to part with the army. Wang Jianlin, however, showed no hesitation. At that time, it was not uncommon for leaders in Wang Jianlin's position to take up a similar job in the private sector. Wang Jianlin pondered his choices, yet he did not change his mind. The reason he was prepared to risk transferring to a civilian job was that he knew that the order had been issued with a bigger picture in mind. Furthermore, he trusted that even if he was transferred to a local job, he could still do well.

With these thoughts in mind, Wang Jianlin decisively shed the army uniform that he had worn for 17 years. Although the iron barracks did not possess the lure to keep the talented Wang Jianlin, he had got a lot out of his 17-year military career. The army toned his body, tempered his will, strengthened his character and established a sense of integrity. He learned not to fear any difficulties and found the courage to dive into studying, which greatly broadened his knowledge. He gained the skills to deal with problems head on. All the skills that he learned in the army were precious to him. It could even be said that these skills proved to be a powerful guarantee for his later achievements with Wanda.

Wang Jianlin's life after he left the army was not easy, but the soldier's blood that flowed in his veins always motivated him to carry on until he built up, step by step, his own Wanda Empire.

CHAPTER

A REAL ESTATE EMPIRE

FIRST STEPS

After Wang Jianlin left the army, he was not immediately swept away by waves of entrepreneurship. He carefully reviewed his options and considered the governmental connections he had amassed during his time in the army. But in the end, he decided to enter the political field.

Wang Jianlin's achievements during his army career were considerable and he was seen as an outstanding soldier. Surely, then, there was a place for him in the civil service. He became head of the Xigang district government in Dalian city.

Dalian is a pleasant coastal city and the office environment was also very agreeable. On his first day at work, Wang Jianlin hadn't even had enough time to familiarize himself with the workings of the office or to meet with important officials before lunchtime arrived. He noticed that many of his colleagues ate out. He thought this a bit strange and enquired from one of his colleagues why people did not eat in a canteen. He was told that the government did not provide a canteen.

Enquiring further, he gathered that it was not that the government did not wish to build a canteen – building one was easy, but the difficulty was supplying gas. The relevant departments in the district government had not completed the required procedures for using gas. When it came to central heating, the district government was equivalent to an unregistered household without a residence permit.

This did not strike Wang Jianlin as an especially difficult task. All that needed to be done was to comply with the regulations of the liquefaction plant. Once the necessary procedures were completed, there was no reason why the problem could not be solved. He went to a lot trouble to contact the head engineer who was in charge of gas fittings and enquire about the problem. To his surprise, as soon the engineer heard 'Xigang district government' he involuntarily started shaking his head and refused to listen to Wang Jianlin. Having suffered rejection on multiple occasions, Wang Jianlin could not help wondering why the head engineer behaved in this way.

There was no further development regarding this matter for some time, yet Wang Jianlin did not give up hope. Whenever he had time he would head over to the engineer's work unit. Even if he was turned away, Wang Jianlin refused to get angry. He was determined to resolve the gas problem no matter what. After several failed attempts, Wang Jianlin managed to find out the engineer's home address from the clerks in his work unit. He then proceeded to call on him at home. As soon as the engineer saw Wang Jianlin, he slammed the door shut with a loud thump. Wang Jianlin was not angry. He persevered in his efforts and in the end the engineer was moved by his sincerity. The next time Wang Jianlin came to call on him, he finally revealed the root of the problem.

When the district government offices were built, the relevant officer had contacted this engineer about gas fitting. It so happened that the engineer was busy with other matters, or perhaps he came across as slightly cold. Unexpectedly, the district government officer flew into a rage and turned nasty. From that moment on, this engineer held a grudge. Later on, the two sides met several times to discuss this matter face-to-face, but whenever they were reminded of the ill feelings from their first meeting, the discussion came to a dead end. From then on, the mutual rage simmered.

The engineer shared his grievance with Wang Jianlin, and the long overdue completion of the gas fitting procedure was quickly resolved under Wang Jianlin's guidance. Wang Jianlin did not stop at that. He returned to his former trade and took on a post that he had once assumed in the army: he put himself in charge of procurement for the district government canteen. He drew on the financial and management knowledge he had gained during his time in the army. First, he introduced cost limits on procurement. Once the costs were under control, he dedicated the savings to improving the quality of food for his colleagues. This won him universal approval. It was also the first opportunity since he had left the army to demonstrate his skills at economic management.

By 1988, Wang Jianlin had been deputy head of the Xigang district government for two years. He had familiarized himself with the government's working procedures and he had established good interpersonal relationships within the organization.

At this time, a residential property development company that was a subsidiary of the Xigang district government was causing much concern among the government's officials. For historical reasons, coupled with the fact that at that time there was no widespread understanding of how to do business, the district government had failed to achieve any remarkable successes in developing the company. This was despite the fact that they had replaced the general manager on multiple occasions in an effort to stimulate development. Instead, the constant changes of management had seemingly turned this company into a small boat tossed about by the wind and rain. With several million yuan of debt, it had become a hot potato for the district government.

In the late 1980s and early 1990s, several million yuan was considered an astronomical figure. One can only imagine what kind of state a district-level company must have been in to incur such a debt. It could be said that the company was on the verge of bankruptcy. But, since the company had been established by the district government, it would have been a public scandal if it really had been allowed to go bankrupt. After weighing up their options multiple times, the district government was at a loss and could only open the position to outside talent. Wang Jianlin, just as the army announced the '1 million disarmament order', volunteered to be made general manager of the residential property development company.

Not only could many of his friends and colleagues not comprehend his behaviour, but even the head of the Xigang district government was astonished and regarded his wish with both hope and fear.

What made the government hopeful was that Wang Jianlin's work record had been excellent from the moment he joined the organization. Wang Jianlin could also act as the government's unofficial troubleshooter. If he was offering to clear up the mess that the residential housing company was in, it might turn out to be a similar success story to the building of the canteen. Wang Jianlin was bold, yet at the same time well acquainted with government intricacies.

What they were fearful of was that if Wang Jianlin accepted this hot-potato case and failed – like countless others before him who had arrived full of excitement only to return with ashen hair and muddy faces – it was bound to have a negative impact on his future career. Also, if he left, the internal department would lose a valuable worker. What, in the end, was the right thing to do?

You can't have your cake and eat it, too. The district government leaders weighed up their options time and time again and also consulted Wang Jianlin on several occasions. In the end, they agreed that Wang Jianlin was to be general manager of the residential housing development company.

To make a real change, one must start by changing the way people think. If Wang Jianlin wanted to change the company, he first had to change his way of thinking as well as his way of doing things. He set about making drastic changes in the company. He conscientiously studied the management rules. Whenever he came across a clause that was illogical or hindered the development of the business, he immediately altered it or deleted it altogether. The firmness and speed with which he carried out these reforms came from the iron will of a soldier, embedded in his bones.

Inspired by his own innovative thinking, Wang Jianlin actively encouraged workers to take the initiative and think outside the box. He succeeded in pulling the Xigang district residential housing development company from stagnation to revitalization.

During the same year, Wang Jianlin also took on another residential housing development project in Nanshan. His reform plan played an important role in this project.

Up until then, Xigang residential housing projects had a reputation for construction delays and poor quality, resulting from lack of motivation and lethargy on the part of the employees. Consequently, many people were dissatisfied with the company's performance.

But Wang Jianlin was a newcomer to the real estate industry. Although the Nanshan project brought in considerable revenue under his leadership and was a major win for the company, it was still insignificant compared to the size of the company's debt. It did not take long for Wang Jianlin to make yet another surprising move. He accepted a developmental project that many of his predecessors had either looked down on or were too afraid to tackle – the development of the old city of Dalian.

Many of his colleagues in the real estate industry mocked him for this decision. They said that after his taste of success with the Nanshan project, he was too sure that luck was on his side, and knew no boundaries. The Xigang district government leaders held their breath at his decision. They were not confident that Wang Jianlin could surprise them once again.

Wang Jianlin had once more arrived at a crumbling mess of a situation and was determined to put it right. With public opinion resolutely against his decision, he was unwilling to let go of this business opportunity and in the end decided to stand his ground and fight. As for any question regarding profit, he had the following answer: first build the houses, then sell each square metre for a couple of hundred yuan more than usual. In this way, all problems would naturally be resolved. And so he led the workers of the Xigang residential housing development company to rise to the challenge. He encouraged his employees, saying: "If we can sell the houses at ¥1,500 per square metre, we can earn profit." Faced with this estimate, many of the workers expressed doubt. Wang Jianlin was, however, very optimistic. He believed that by being proactive and thinking of a solution, he would come up with a way of making the price shoot up and everything would work out.

Propelled by a sense of urgency, Wang Jianlin repeatedly consulted his team. They studied information relevant to the real estate industry and in the end decided to put into practice the following four innovations:

First, promote high-rise housing. In those days, there was no concept of high-rise housing in Dalian city. The Xigang district residential housing development company was hoping to make this into a point of attraction for consumers by building 30-floor high-rise tower blocks. Later on, these high-rise tower blocks would be called 'Wanda high-rises' (The Xigang district residential housing development company was later renamed Dalian Wanda Group Co. Ltd).

Next, innovate in design. The company not only promoted large units of over 130 square metres; it also led the way in constructing living rooms with outside-facing windows of aluminium alloy. At that time almost none of the real estate companies were promoting overly large apartments. Neither was there a distinction between outside-facing windows and interior ones.

Thirdly, build a bathroom roughly 5 square metres in area in each apartment. In those days, not every residence was equipped with a separate bathroom. The majority of people had to hold their noses and put up with the smell of public toilets. It was only people of high standing, such as county officials, who could live in residences with private bathrooms. In this respect, Wang Jianlin was a pioneer.

Lastly, install anti-theft doors. This was at a time when the Panpan Group was introducing security doors which sold for just ¥80-90 per piece. Wang Jianlin considered these doors to be sturdier than the traditional wooden doors and yet the production cost was no higher. That is why he decided to fit each apartment with a set of these doors. Once fitted, the whole apartment had an entirely different look. This too was a major innovation in those days.

Apart from the above-mentioned selling points, Wang Jianlin also chose a unique approach to marketing. At first he wanted to rely on newspaper advertising, but he was soon met with a challenge: there were only two official newspapers for the whole city and the space for advertising was extremely limited.

After some consideration, Wang Jianlin chose a different approach: why not discuss the possibility of working together with the television station? Hong Kong and Taiwan TV dramas were just starting to take off at that time, so Wang Jianlin thought that if he could cut in with adverts at the start and in the middle of each episode, he was bound to get good exposure. And so it was. He contacted the TV station and secured advertising slots, so when the series was broadcast, many city dwellers saw Wang Jianlin's housing estate adverts.

The housing conditions in Dalian city in the 1980s were relatively poor. Wang Jianlin thought long and hard and in the end managed to greatly improve the standard of living conditions just by altering a few simple things. This was a welcome change for the citizens of Dalian, and the financial rewards were sizeable. Even more importantly, apart from the considerable revenue, this project also established good relations between Wang Jianlin and the government.

RESTRUCTURING AND THE BIRTH OF WANDA

Wang Jianlin knew that behind the awesome success of his residential housing construction scheme was the toil and sweat of his employees. Although the company as a whole earned a huge profit, the hard-working employees had no way of sharing this prize, as in those times Wang Jianlin had no control over rewarding his employees. However, in order to let all employees enjoy the company's achievements, he decided to organize a company outing during the May Day holiday.

The next day, however, the atmosphere was soured: accusations were made to the Dalian City Disciplinary Commission, reporting Wang Jianlin for abusing public funds and indulging in extravagant eating and drinking. He who has a mind to beat his dog will easily find his stick! This accusation could have put Wang Jianlin in serious trouble, as abuse of public funds was considered a very grave offence. The central government was at that very time investigating embezzlement and corruption. Although what Wang Jianlin did could not be considered embezzlement, it could, however, be construed as displaying certain characteristics of corruption. On this basis the Dalian City Disciplinary Commission was inclined to give Wang Jianlin a strict punishment in the form of a disciplinary warning, or by circulating a notice of criticism.

After a period of mediation with the staff of the Xigang District Municipal Party Committee, the Dalian Disciplinary Commission made some concessions. One member of the Commission said: "Since Wang Jianlin's behaviour is understandable, we decided not to subject him to an official warning or circulation of criticism, but he must inevitably be criticized as a form of warning, in order to prevent a similar offence happening in the future. Furthermore, the ¥200 per person cost of the company outing that was taken from public funds shall be compensated in full by the employees of the Xigang District Residential Housing Development Company."

The matter was thus laid to rest, but Wang Jianlin himself could not rest. He thought that since his employees made great contributions to the company, they should be rewarded accordingly. If there was no system of rewards, where would employees get their motivation? He also pondered about other problems the company ' was facing. The longer he pondered, the more helpless he felt. He had a feverish desire to bring about change. This was the moment when the root of Wanda's restless future took hold.

Xigang District Residential Housing Development Company was connected to the Xigang district government and therefore counted as a state-owned enterprise. In those times the organizational structure inherent in state-owned enterprises acted in many ways like shackles to the development of the enterprise. Once Wang Jianlin had assumed the post of general manager of the Xigang District Residential Housing Development Company, he frequently came across a number of practical difficulties.

The first problem was that Wang Jianlin had no control over the employment and dismissal of his employees, nor did he have authority to appoint and remove cadres (Communist Party activists within the organization).

The second problem was that he had no decision-making powers over the distribution of monetary reward according to the employees' contribution to the company.

Serving as the head of the company and yet not being able to distribute wages based on the allocation of work was an embarrassment. Wang Jianlin could no longer put up with being used as a figurehead, a mere puppet. After detailed analysis, he saw that the company's organizational structure was at the heart of the problem. If he wished to change the company from the bottom up, he had to start by changing its structure.

Just as Wang Jianlin was mulling over how to change the Xigang District Residential Housing Development Company's structure, exciting news spread through the city: the State Commission for Restructuring the Economic System and the Dalian City Commission for Restructuring the Economic System decided that three enterprises in Dalian would be appointed as the first pilot joint-stock companies in north-east China. This was in 1992.

When Wang Jianlin heard the news, he was beside himself with joy. He spotted his opportunity and took the initiative to apply for consideration. The State Commission for Restructuring the Economic System and the Dalian City Commission for Restructuring the Economic System took note of Wang Jianlin's enthusiasm. Many state-owned enterprises had no desire to change. On top of everything, Wang Jianlin's company had a strong record of good performance, which is why he was given one of the three places. And so Wang Jianlin won an opportunity to carry out a thorough structural reform within the company. This was one of the decisive winning moments of his career. Xigang District Residential Housing Development Company was thereafter renamed Dalian Wanda Group Co. Ltd.

Once state-owned shares had been replaced by private financing, Wang Jianlin had full control of the company and became its rightful owner. This was a historic change. Looking at it from today's point of view, we cannot emphasize Wang Jianlin's structural reform enough. From then on, Wanda was rid of governmental constraints and could venture into the wide ocean of commerce at Wang Jianlin's will, bound only by the forces of the market.

The change of name had significantly more far-reaching consequences than might appear at first sight. After all, the entire structural organization changed along with the system of power distribution. The renamed Dalian Wanda Group Co. Ltd. would never again be subject to official constraints. It was about to grow wings and fly to freedom. As for Wang Jianlin, he now embarked on a path of Wanda development that belonged to him.

Once the process of restructuring was successfully completed, Wanda became a platform for Wang Jianlin to live out his dreams. Inexperienced in the commercial field yet brimming with ambition, Wang Jianlin followed the then popular trend and tried to diversify his activities. He invested in pharmaceutical companies, the elevator industry, and even in transformer substation equipment. However, due to a lack of partners or a sufficient level of specialization, all of these industries and investments ended in failure.

The temporary loss of profit caused by diversification made him see the value of focusing on a single industry. That is why he rejected the suggestion to buy and invest in coal mines in Inner Mongolia. He solidly focused on the familiar real estate field. Thanks to his plentiful connections in Dalian city and his ever-increasing experience and capital, Wanda Group was thriving in the real estate industry and gradually became the top property developer in Dalian.

With rapid development came an increasing number of problems; this was a critical period during which the enterprise was put to the test. At the start of 1996, even though Wang Jianlin's business was undergoing steady development, he took extra precautions and led the way among nationwide real estate enterprises in proposing three guarantees aimed at tackling the widespread problems of undersized apartments, fraudulent sales and inferior quality in the industry. The three guarantees were: no leakage, adequate apartment size, and free refunds in the event of dissatisfaction.

The three guarantees policy was very controversial and had a far-reaching impact on the Chinese real estate market. Dalian city government even issued a formal document calling upon the city construction system to learn from Wanda Group. As one might expect, Wang Jianlin's enormous influence brought him great success.

By 1998, Wanda Group's sales in Dalian city added up to ¥30 billion, which equalled 25% of real estate sales in the whole city. The Wanda empire slowly started to emerge from among the hubbub.

HIS FIRST COUP IN COMMERCIAL REAL ESTATE

From the moment the Xigang District Residential Housing Development Company changed its name to Dalian Wanda Group Co. Ltd., it set out on a developmental road of exploration. From 1995 to 1998, Wanda Group relied on its network of people as well as its capital to step into other industries besides real estate, such as pharmaceuticals and elevators. Unfortunately, such endeavours came to a rapid end. Nonetheless, these momentary setbacks did not diminish Wang Jianlin's confidence.

The reason Wang Jianlin persisted in developing business in new industries was partly that he wanted Wanda to gain long-term, stable income, and partly because he was acutely aware of business intelligence. He thought that if Wanda only relied on real estate it was unlikely to get far.

Wang Jianlin discovered that although the real estate industry had bright prospects, there were disadvantages to it that could not be overlooked. The cash flow was irregular. During times when new units were being sold, the company had access to a steady flow of cash, but once a housing complex had been sold off, the company's cash flow would decrease as new land had to be bought. Based on this simple consideration of profit, Wanda had to carry on its search to ensure a steady flow of income. It was only in 2000 that Wanda decided to turn commercial real estate into its pillar industry.

On 17 May 2000 came the crucial board meeting at which Wang Jianlin rolled out his plan for vigorous development of the commercial real estate sector. This proved to be a major turning point in the group's history. Wang Jianlin explained that the income from selling a residence is a one-off profit, yet commercial properties can be both sold and let out. They can also be self-operated. In this way it is possible to gain long-term profits.

Looking at it from the point of view of development, Wang Jianlin was thinking along the right track. It was a shame that not everyone shared his talent for foresight. Some in Wanda Group were not ready to subscribe to his view. Many founding members expressed their opinions and simply maintained that the commercial real estate plan was not suitable for current development and would only cause trouble.

Wang Jianlin stood his ground in the face of doubt and incomprehension. In reality, he, too, was at times hesitant. His predecessors had sought in the past to pioneer the business of commercial real estate, but most failed and turned back. But in Wang Jianlin's mind, if Wanda wanted to expand beyond Dalian and become a global franchise enterprise, then it was inevitable that it would need to take on high-end commercial property projects.

In the end, the stubborn Wang Jianlin decided to allow five years for the transition to take effect. If by 2005 Wanda saw no signs of improvement, the project was to be immediately abandoned. Wang Jianlin wanted to give himself an opportunity, but even more importantly he wanted his team to be faced with a tough challenge.

After the decision to carry out full transition to the commercial real estate sector, the first product to be promoted was the Wanda high-rise. This was a type of detached high-rise office building or apartment block that was to be put up for sale. The first three floors were rented out and turned into commercial plazas. In those days, Wanda had very limited sources of commercial tenants; the majority were made up of small shops and restaurants. Due to the fact that businesses of all sizes were often tardy in paying their rent, Wang Jianlin was forced to set up a team specifically dedicated to collecting rent. The process was troublesome and inefficient and the returns were far from what he had hoped for.

In order to find a way out of this awkward predicament, Wang Jianlin came up with a new idea and decided to work with more powerful and influential tenants. He proposed a motto, 'Rent to the Global Fortune 500', in order to achieve this. At that time Wal-Mart had only recently arrived in China and urgently needed a marketplace to expand its reach. Wanda could use Wal-Mart's popularity and influence to open up new prospects.

After a series of negotiations, the vice-president of Wal-Mart was still in no way prepared to agree easily; Wang

Jianlin was at a loss. After several twists and turns he managed to get through to Wal-Mart's chief executive officer (CEO) for Asia-Pacific, Joe Hatfield. After another round of consultations, Hatfield somewhat reservedly said that it was too early to speak of strategic cooperation, but they might as well first give it a go and see.

And so it was. The two parties spent over half a year in dozens of negotiations. In the end, Wal-Mart agreed to work with Wanda and the first Wanda Plaza was built in the city of Changchun in Jilin province. This was considered to be a coup for Wanda.

CONTRACT STRATEGY

Wanda's success in the commercial real estate project was dependent on what Wang Jianlin termed the 'contract commercial real estate' strategic marketing model. It relied on first signing a tenancy contract with well-known businesses, and only then building shopping malls. This marketing model greatly reduced the risk inherent in business.

Initially, before he managed to get Wal-Mart on board for the Wanda Plaza project in Changchun, he was met with one closed door after another. At first, he was not even able to get in touch with Wal-Mart's general manager. However, his unyielding persistence finally won him a meeting with Wal-Mart's executive development deputy director.

Although he eventually got what he was striving for, during their first meeting he could tell that the other party looked down on Wanda. It was only many more meetings later that Wang Jianlin got Wal-Mart's reluctant approval for cooperation. The first step was to find a suitable place. When Wal-Mart's development director heard that Wang

Jianlin had chosen Changchun as the location for the new Wanda Plaza, he at once rejected the notion. His reason was that when Wal-Mart chose locations in the US, it would only ever consider the suburbs. It was out of the question to choose a location in the city, let alone in the city centre.

Wang Jianlin had his own opinion on the matter and was unwilling to let it go. In the end, he personally called on Wal-Mart's chief executive officer for Asia-Pacific to describe to him Wanda's concrete conception of the plan. Having listened to Wang Jianlin's vision, Wal-Mart's chief executive officer considered it highly feasible. He thereupon visited Changchun to examine the proposed location and gave the go-ahead. And so the Changchun Wanda Plaza was successfully opened.

In truth, Wang Jianlin had anticipated that his plan would be successful, but he had never imagined that the Changchun Wanda Plaza would prove to be so popular. And Wal-Mart, upon seeing the result, swallowed its pride and decided to sign contracts for five more city-centre stores.

The painstakingly won collaboration agreement with Wal-Mart gradually revealed its inherent value. Wal-Mart was the flagship store in the new Wanda Plaza. With its wide variety of goods, pleasant environment and trustworthy brands, it quickly gained popularity with consumers.

Wal-Mart's change of course had an immediate effect on other businesses. It is said that at the start of Wal-Mart's collaboration with Wanda, Wal-Mart was given half of the rent for free. The success of the Changchun Wanda Plaza, however, allowed other businesses to see the great potential for profit, which is why, one after the other, they hurried to work with Wanda.

Initially, Wanda's agreement with Wal-Mart was perhaps slightly unfavourable for Wanda, but one must not underestimate the advertising potential inherent in this collaboration. Furthermore, along with Wanda's development, its standing in relation to Wal-Mart also imperceptibly started changing. This was in no small measure due to Wang Jianlin's practical understanding that a little can be sacrificed for a lot to be gained.

As Wanda continued in its development, the businesses that wanted to collaborate with the company became ever more diversified. For example, apart from Wal-Mart, there were other supermarkets including Carrefour, Tesco, China Resources Vanguard and others. The majority of the businesses were even willing to give up their right to choose a location, as long as Wanda collaborated with them. In other words, no matter where Wanda decided to build a Wanda Plaza, they would sign a contract for that location.

Having worked in the commercial real estate industry for some years, Wang Jianlin was well acquainted with it and used his knowledge to optimize the distribution of different types of businesses. For example, in every Wanda Plaza in a major city, the food and drink stores were always located on the top floor. This was also one of his innovations. He even invented a name for his theory, 'waterfall effect'. According to his analysis, a characteristic of Chinese people is that they love good food. If all kinds of delicacies were grouped together and located on the top floor, the Chinese were willing to run all the way up just for the food. On their way down they were bound to walk past other stores, which increased the customers' overall retention time. It was just like a waterfall, flowing down from the top.

As a result of Wanda's long-term collaboration deal with Wal-Mart, the 'contract strategy' gradually became better established. By the time a new Wanda Plaza was ready to be built, details concerning the tenant of the flagship store were already resolved. Over half of all the area available for rent was already taken up by tenants. During the operations on the ground, Wang Jianlin retained a people-centred approach. He would first find out the exact requirements of the tenants and then suit the plaza to their needs. A key to success in the commercial real estate sector was that one first and foremost had to think of one's customers. Only when the tenants were able to make a profit would Wanda make a profit.

Wanda's 'commercial real estate contract model' quickly achieved the goal of breathing life into the surrounding areas. It turned the Wanda Plazas' localities into the new beating hearts of the city. It was reported that such new city centres enjoyed 80,000 to 150,000 visitors each day and even close to 300,000 in busy periods. This significantly boosted consumer demand and resulted in increasingly bustling and flourishing cities.

Later on, this kind of commercial real estate contract model became key to Wanda's competitiveness. Wang Jianlin proudly stated that the contract real estate model was quickly imitated by others in the commercial real estate sector, but none managed to match Wanda.

INDUSTRY MAKEOVER

In the process of continuous development, Wanda relied on Dalian and eventually became Dalian's jewel of residential real estate. From there it started its expansion to the national level. Wang Jianlin grasped decisive opportunities and made sure that Wanda stood out from the crowd, becoming a renowned national property developer with great influence.

In reality, Wang Jianlin had long before already set his eyes on expanding to the entire country. As early as 1993, he attempted to start a developmental real estate project in the southern city of Guangzhou. In those days it was still extremely rare to see private real estate enterprises operate on a national scale. The industry and commerce department in Guangzhou was unwilling to process the registration for a branch company of Wanda Group. Wang Jianlin was forced to develop his business through a development company run by overseas Chinese. Although the process was gruelling, it had always been Wang Jianlin's dream to go nationwide.

What really made Wanda's national expansion possible was its commercial real estate model. From 2001 onwards, Wanda Group became a spearhead in expanding across the country in the commercial real estate sector, storming countless city centres. The concrete manifestations were in the form of the Wanda high-rises or Wanda Plazas. Each high-rise or plaza was accompanied by a large-scale supermarket, cinema chain, stores and restaurants. Thanks to Wanda's strength in commercial real estate, what had been a newcomer to the commercial world finally began to show what it was capable of.

We can identify three distinct commercial products during Wanda Group's development process.

The first stage of commercial real estate development was characterized by the single-store model. As the name implies, it consisted of a single building that housed all the businesses. The total area was about 50,000 to 60,000 square metres. The actual construction process was as follows: first a commercial high-rise was built. Wanda Group opened up boutique stores on the ground floor. The supermarket was on the first floor. The second floor was devoted to furniture stores and the third floor was taken up by the cinema. Representatives of this model are the Wanda Plazas in Changchun, Qingdao and Nanjing.

There was an upgrade in the second generation of plazas known as 'combined stores'. These were produced between 2003 and 2005. They were made up of a number of separate stores. The total area averaged between 100,000 and 150,000 square metres. They housed around ten different types of businesses including stores, supermarkets and cinemas. Representatives of this model are the Wanda Plazas in Tianjin, Nanning and Wuhan.

In order to attract more consumers, Wanda Group started to experiment with diversification of businesses during this period, continuously introducing new types of entertainment in the form of video-game stores, department stores and restaurants. Even more importantly, Wanda started to lay emphasis on the scale of its commercial real estate.

The third generation was the Wanda city complex, also called HOPSCA – H for hotel, O for office building, P for public space, S for shopping mall, C for culture and recreation, and A for apartment. This kind of city complex is Wanda Group's key product on the market. It is a one-stop development that comprehensively caters to all the consumer's needs. It is the equivalent of building a new city centre. Representatives of this model are the Wanda Plazas in Shanghai, Beijing, Ningbo and Chengdu.

The third-generation commercial model of the Wanda Plaza also includes an indoor pedestrian street lined with well-known brands. Grouping major businesses together in this way was a significant innovation in the design of commercial real estate space.

During the five years between Wanda's decision to turn to the commercial real estate sector in 2000 and the launching of Wanda's city complex in 2005, Wanda Group accomplished a neat makeover. It can be objectively said that by 2005 Wanda Group already enjoyed high popularity across the whole country. By that time the third-generation model of the Wanda Plaza had reached maturity. However, among nationwide property developers, Wanda's power and influence was far behind that of Vanke, a residential real estate company based in Shenzhen, in Guangdong province. Even Country Garden Holdings, also based in Guangdong province, was in a stronger position than Wanda, though it had only appeared on the market in 2007. Nonetheless, Wang Jianlin's superior financing capacity ensured Wanda Group's continued rapid expansion. By 2007, Wanda Group already boasted dozens of Wanda Plazas nationwide. It was at the forefront of the commercial real estate sector.

The US subprime mortgage crisis struck in 2008 and greatly decreased Chinese exports. The central government decided to resort to a fiscal expansion policy to stimulate the development of the economy. The state put aside ¥4 trillion to inject into the economy. At that time the monetary policy was relatively relaxed. Adding to the wide impact of the crisis, local governments were keen to quickly convert their land into money. Similarly, banks hoped to see more customers take out large loans.

At that time, the China Banking Regulatory Commission conducted monthly checks on the banks' lending quotas to see whether or not they had reached the baseline. Consequently, when large real estate developers applied for loans, they would generally succeed without much ado.

Wang Jianlin immediately grabbed this historic opportunity for expansion. When he mentioned the 2008 crisis in an interview later on, he said: "Will there be another such opportunity in the future? Many people were scared by the outlook of the events and did not dare to agree to new projects. At the beginning of 2009, Wanda, on the other hand, seized another dozen new projects. The price of land was so low it made one wonder."

The US subprime mortgage crisis negatively affected numerous industries across the world. However, Wang Jianlin used it to achieve rapid development for his company. Wanda's development during this period was remarkable: Wang Jianlin managed to overtake large enterprises that were previously ahead of Wanda, and leave them in his wake, an astonishing feat.

Wanda's rapid growth during this period, as well as its trademark Wanda city complex model, were in agreement with the expectations of local governments. Wanda's complex developmental model, which emphasized injecting a lot of business into a large plot of land, had an extraordinary effect in stimulating the local economy. Wanda Plazas also attracted many Chinese as well as international premium brands. In many cases the Plazas improved the overall outlook of the whole city, which is why local governments were highly motivated to seek collaboration with Wanda Group.

Following Wanda's collaboration with local governments, the scale of the group's projects continued to increase. The total area increased from hundreds of hectares to thousands, the built-up area went up from dozens of square metres to hundreds of thousands of square metres, and the amount of investment skyrocketed from dozens of billions of yuan to hundreds on hundreds of billions. New concepts such as shopping malls, shopping centres, culture and travel holiday resorts, among others, continued to enrich the Wanda model. And so, Wanda's fourth-generation commercial product – the Wanda City – gradually started to take form.

THE WANDA MODEL

Wanda Group marketed itself with a well-known catchphrase: "Wanda Plaza – the key to a vibrant city centre". This catchphrase reflected Wanda's influence and skill in constructing city centres. Thanks to its competitive advantage, Wanda Group has the freedom to choose suitable locations for rapidly building Wanda Plazas in second-, third- and fourth-tier cities. Currently, Wanda Group is swiftly expanding across the whole country at an average rate of 20 Wanda Plazas per year.

By doing so, Wanda has not only ensured generation of profits through the speedy success of its brand, but also introduced the Wanda model to consumers across different cities. Each of Wanda's unique strategic development models has deeply influenced the respective cities' commercial development.

A classic example is Yinchuan, a tier-two city with a population of just over 2 million. Wanda Group invested in three real estate projects, putting forward a total of ¥7.5 billion of funds over the course of three years. In total, two commercial city complexes were built. Considering that Yinchuan was not a tier-one city, what explains Wanda's earnest interest in it? The answer lies in the city dwellers' hunger for a city complex.

In 2011, a Wanda Plaza was opened in the Jinfeng district of Yinchuan city. In the first four days after opening, a record number of more than 800,000 visits was achieved. This naturally had the effect of urging Wanda to continue investing in such fertile ground.

By 2012, the Jinfeng Wanda Plaza had a turnover of ¥800 million. In just one year, it had become the plaza with the fastest-growing turnover out of more than 70 other Wanda Plazas across the country. The Wanda Plaza in the Xixia district of Yinchuan witnessed a stream of over 690,000 visits in just two days after going into operation. Its revenue reached ¥39 million.

It was in 2006 that Wanda Group built its landmark structure in Yinchuan for the first time: the Wanda Oriental Red cinema city. At that time, it was a historic event that brought more and more people back to the cinema screens. Recently, it has formed part of Wanda's strategy for entering a new city. During the first stage, Wanda gradually moves its brand to the forefront of the local consumers' consciousness by building a cinema or a shopping mall. In the next step, Wanda then brings in a Wanda Plaza or even a Wanda city complex.

Customers soon noticed that when the Wanda cinema city opened in the Oriental Red Plaza, there was already a base structure for a Wanda city complex on the way.

According to the Wanda convention, the Wanda city complexes grouped commerce, business, accommodation and other functions in one place. They provided a one-stop shopping, catering, fitness, relaxation, entertainment and office-building service.

As expected, the Jinfeng district Wanda Plaza opened within five years. Eating, drinking, entertainment, travel, amusement and shopping facilities fully met consumers' leisure and recreation needs. The accompanying hotel-style apartments and office buildings catered to consumers' requirements for a working environment.

The Jinfeng district Wanda Plaza has thrived since its opening. Yearly revenue rose at a rate of almost ¥200 million per year from 2012 to 2014 – from ¥800 million to ¥1.1 billion and ¥1.3 billion.

To a certain extent, Yinchuan's commercial outlook has become diversified due to the appearance of Wanda, which was of great benefit both to Yinchuan city and to Wanda Group.

And so Wang Jianlin, through his replication of a commercial real estate strategy, succeeded in expanding the Wanda Plaza from one location to the entire country. He then ceaselessly worked on making it take root and flourish. Rather than looking at it as a form of Wang Jianlin's conservative expansion, it is better to see it as his neverending confidence in the Wanda model. He believed that as long as the Wanda brand was there, it did not matter where he expanded, as he was bound to attract a large crowd of consumers.

3

CHAPTER

DESTINED FOR FOOTBALL

THE WANDA TEAM

In 1994, Wanda Group had only been in existence for a few years and was still in the initial phases of its development. The public began to take more notice of it at this time because of the Dalian Wanda Football Club, which it set up.

Dalian Wanda FC served to acquaint the outside world with Wanda, but it also sought people's approval for the Wanda brand. Some might perhaps have wondered why Wang Jianlin chose to set up a football club at a time when his efforts in real estate were not paying off. Others doubted the motive for setting up the club: was it a pilot programme as part of a football reform, or was it a magnificent business turnaround for Wanda Group?

In China, Dalian citizens' love for football was plain for everybody to see. The majority of players on the national football team came from Dalian. It could be said that Dalian was a repository for aspiring national team players. Conversely, if the national team was not playing well, the players from Dalian were the first to be blamed.

As soon as the go-ahead for reform was announced, Dalian football fans moved into action. They broke away from the professional league system and local football associations and started exploring the possibilities of setting up new clubs.

As early as 1991, at the national working conference on football, Gai Zengsheng, a well-known former national team player who at that time was vice-chairman of the Chinese Football Association and head of Dalian City Sports Commission, proposed his vision of establishing 'special football zones' during a small-group discussion. His idea was supported by municipal leaders in charge of sport development.

When the national team was defeated in Kuala Lumpur two months later, the Dalian City Sports Commission officially submitted a report on establishing a special football zone to the National Sports Commission. On 8 May, the Sports Commission approved the document and agreed to allow Dalian to establish a special football zone. Wang Jianlin, who had always been on good terms with the Sports Commission, undoubtedly saw an opportunity in this. His capital was acutely needed for setting up a special football zone. Once the club was set up, the Wanda business would become a principal part of the club and media broadcasts would serve to expose the brand to increased advertising. All these were platforms that Wanda could rely on during its expansion. And so, ¥4 million of sponsorship turned Wanda into a primary potential partner for the Dalian Sports Commission that was just making preparations for founding a football club. On 8 March 1994, just over a month before the start of the competition season in the professional league, Dalian Wanda FC was formally established.

Dalian Wanda FC players were already very accomplished to start with. With Wanda's abundant funding, they were unstoppable: they won eight times in a row. The considerable economic strength of the team played an important part in these victories. Wanda Group did everything in its power to allow the players to focus on football 100%. For example, when the players were staying in dormitories next to the pitch, Wanda renovated the accommodation in order for them to train with peace of mind. Wanda not only replaced the floor, they also fitted the rooms with air-conditioning.

During the final of the Jia A League in 1994, Dalian Wanda FC took on the local host club, Sichuan Quanxing

FC. Sichuan Quanxing had never lost a match, and were keen to keep up the record on their home turf. Similarly, Dalian Wanda FC were not willing to lose, so they focused all their efforts on the game.

Half an hour into the match, Dalian Wanda FC were already winning 3-0. Thanks to Wanda's unending string of victories, even the fans of the Sichuan team began to shout the slogan "Kick it in, Wanda". In the end, Dalian Wanda FC became the champions of a professional league for the first time.

Hong Kong Television broadcast the Jia A League final live to over 50 countries and territories. Dalian Wanda FC's performance left a deep impression on football fans around the world.

After Dalian Wanda FC came out victorious, the director of the National Sports Commission, Wu Shaozu, congratulated them on their success. It goes without saying that Dalian Wanda FC's victory was closely linked to Wanda Group's investment in the team.

Naturally, Wanda Group gained some invisible benefits as a result of the victory, which increased the reputation and popularity of the Wanda brand. Although Dalian Wanda FC retired after six years, this had no negative effect on the brand.

Wang Jianlin was undoubtedly right to invest in football. Although the football reform in China was only at an experimental stage and both Wang Jianlin and Wanda became targets of experiment, Wanda Group gained a considerable reputation because of this.

FOOTBALL AS BUSINESS

Wang Jianlin was himself a devout football fan. He described himself as "never missing a game" during the World Cup. He would set an alarm to avoid missing key matches.

What he regretted most was that the Chinese team did not compete in the World Cup. He quoted this as the reason for sponsoring the Dalian football team, saying: "A few years ago the company did not have the means for this. Now that we have some money, we will naturally make ourselves seen. A 4-million-yuan yearly investment is just the start ... As the company matures, we will increase our investment."

Unfortunately, Wang Jianlin's regret was not resolved as a direct result of his complete devotion to football. It was only at the 2002 World Cup in Japan and South Korea that Dalian Wanda FC players Hao Haidong, Sun Jihai and Zhang Enhua made their appearance at a World Cup match for the first time. By that time, Wang Jianlin had already left football behind over two years before, and Dalian Wanda FC had been renamed Dalian Shide FC. Nonetheless, having toyed with football for several years, Wang Jianlin clearly saw the benefit that football had brought to him and to his enterprise.

According to the influential newspaper *Southern Weekly*, Wang Jianlin originally put aside only ¥4 million for football investment during the first year. But in the end he got into a serious overspend, adding on a further ¥2 million. Such expenditures were proving to be a heavy burden for Wanda Group, given that it was still in its start-up phase; one could even say that it was virtually killing the company. A director from the Dalian Football Association recollected that upon appraising the situation, Wang Jianlin stated that "that was it", revealing his plans for pulling out of football.

It was only after he met with a cool reception on a visit to Singapore that Wang Jianlin regained his confidence in football promotion.

Accompanied by senior executives, he had visited Singapore to meet with a financial company. They were, however, met with closed doors. With the help of a friend, they let it be known that they were the owners of the champion team of the Jia A league. Only then did the other side lower its defences and treat them with due respect. After his return from Singapore, Wang Jianlin decided to grit his teeth and carry on with the football investment.

In fact, this was not the first time that Wang Jianlin's company had been given the cold shoulder in its attempts to expand outwards. As early as the late 1980s and early 1990s, Wang Jianlin was planning to go to Western Europe. The original plan was to meet up with a senior executive of a certain transnational corporation. The other party was less than pleasant upon seeing Wang Jianlin's documents. The senior executive stated that theirs was a world-renowned company and there were countless other companies who sought to collaborate with them. They had no time and no interest in a company as small as Wang Jianlin's. Should Wang Jianlin be determined to carry on with negotiations, he should first do so with their Beijing branch office.

By the mid-1990s, however, Wanda Group sported the largest neon advert in the world and could proudly say that it had greatly raised the quality of Dalian city centre. It was no longer a 'small company'.

Wang Jianlin had a clear vision for the football club. He was not in it just for fun: he wanted to obtain full control of the club management. He had once described his vision for the club in these terms: "We need to establish enterprise

consciousness through leveraging funds. A radical transformation of the operating mechanism is required. The
club should operate in accordance with football and market
laws. Gradually, we should transform the club into a largely
joint-stock independent legal entity that combines football
and business management in one body and that will eventually stimulate economic growth."

This grew into a classic example of a Western football
club management style, complete with a youth development programme. Other countries with comparably mature
youth development programmes include, among others,
Germany, Spain, France, the US and Japan.

Wang Jianlin, as a chairman of the board, earnestly
watched the team's progress in both home and away games.
As Ren Juyi explained, if there was a match on Sunday,
Wang Jianlin was already on the scene on Saturday. If the
match was on Saturday, Wang Jianlin arrived on Friday. He
was always accompanied by an office director or one of his
subordinates. Not only did he make a habit of attending
each match in person, he also took it on himself to motivate
the players before every match.

Wang Jianlin also took a personal interest in all club hap-
penings, including bringing in foreign players. The Swede
Pelle Blohm was one of the first foreign players in Dalian
Wanda FC. His hair reached down to his shoulders, which
Ren Juyi described as 'womanly'. According to the rules at
the time, players were not allowed to grow long beards or
have long hair.

During the 1996 match season, Blohm was originally
meant to play in the match against Tianjin, but Wanda was
informed before the match that the National Sports Commission had decided that Blohm could not play. The head

of the Chinese Football Association thought that Blohm's hair was too long and had to be cut before he was allowed to play.

There were no scissors in the changing rooms and it looked as though Blohm's hopes for his debut were about to be dashed. Blohm felt that forcing him to cut his hair was ridiculous and so, sighing repeatedly, refused. He wanted Wanda to give up on the international transfer and allow him to return to Sweden. Dalian Wanda FC immediately got on the phone to request further instructions. They managed to obtain temporary permission from senior management for Blohm to play in this match, if he tied his hair up in a ponytail. Upon return to Dalian, however, he was instructed to cut it.

Such rules and regulations on China's part had aggravated Blohm. On their return to Dalian, Wang Jianlin himself visited Blohm at his residence, along with the club's management. They apologized to Blohm and his wife. Wang Jianlin was serious about trying to keep Blohm. He presented him with his own calligraphy collection. In the end, under Wang Jianlin's persuasion, Blohm agreed to stay.

As Ren Juyi described, Wanda persuaded Blohm to symbolically cut his hair shorter by one centimetre. They then gave the hair to the National Sports Commission, saying, "Look, we cut it short: here it is." This was enough to pacify all parties concerned.

Wang Jianlin was clear that fulfilling his duty of care to the club was by itself not sufficient. He understood the importance of monetary reward in motivating professional football players. He tried using bonuses, which existed under the market economy as a way of encouraging the players. To some extent, this has accidentally given rise to the phenomenon of 'money-ridden football'. He said: "What I have been emphasizing from the beginning is that each person's contribution is closely linked to their reward. It is desirable that income becomes further differentiated. The difference between individual players' incomes might be even several dozens of times higher or lower. The monetary reward for those with exceptional performance will be no lower than that of international players. Furthermore, they will have a good post ready for them in the company for when they retire. For those that underperform, we shall take no responsibility for securing them a job after they retire from football."

Wang Jianlin always sought to equate the football industry with a business enterprise. He wanted the players' reward to be equal to their achievements, or even slightly higher than their achievements. The media once reported that no match is complete without seeing Wang Jianlin with his leather suitcase full of millions of yuan.

Apart from cash rewards, Wang Jianlin had a golden football trophy made in order to tap the players' potential. Each of these footballs weighed 300 grams and was made of pure gold. However, it seemed that football players were not very knowledgeable when it came to appreciating quality. They regarded the golden ball as having more of a commemorative value. It was nowhere near as practical a reward as having a luxury car or a house. Wang Jianlin delivered what he had promised and perfected the Wang management style by reverting to luxury cars such as Mercedes-Benz.

Everything he did was intended to motivate the players. This is why he was the first to feel the pressure when the team's results were deteriorating. During the 1995 season,

Wanda lost one match after another. The distraught Wang Jianlin once shared his woes with the media: "It is not easy for a private enterprise like ours to channel ¥1 million a year into football. If I didn't channel this money into football, no one would complain. The profit that gets split among our employees is that much smaller because of the football investment. Not long ago, I heard complaints that the team did not have a transport vehicle. I immediately provided them with one, spending ¥500,000. Recently, I invested a further 2 million into building a training ground jointly with the Shihuishi company. The training ground encompasses two pitches accompanied by a dormitory, complete with private bathrooms and air-conditioning. Last year I agreed to provide three houses for the team, now I have already given five … I have done everything I could from the point of view of a football manager, but I can't win the game on the pitch for them!"

Some people compared Wang Jianlin to the Russian millionaire Roman Abramovich, who ensured that England's Chelsea FC were drowning in money. However, apart from throwing money around to buy players, the two in fact did not have much in common. Wang Jianlin, who was far removed from open-market operations, had started his career more than ten years before Abramovich. His football business was actively supported by Dalian city. The city governors even helped the Wanda team to bring in international talent.

In the football business, dominating the Jia A League was not Wang Jianlin's ultimate aim. His ambitions were set even higher. When he saw that victory in Jia A League was already a sure thing, he revealed that Dalian Wanda FC's next step was to win the Asian Champions League. He hoped to pave a path for Chinese football to dash out of Asia and storm the world. Regrettably, he never achieved his dream.

The closest Dalian Wanda FC came to winning the Asian Champions League was in 1998. In the Asian Champions League final, Dalian Wanda FC met with South Korean Pohang Steelers. The match was very intense. Two hours in, there was no obvious winner or loser, with the score still remaining 0–0. In the end, Wanda lost in the penalty shoot-out and came in second place overall.

BIDDING FAREWELL TO THE PITCH

The local government greatly valued Dalian Wanda FC. However, when it came to actual management, Wanda was always subject to government approval. This kind of limited management frustrated Wang Jianlin. It is reported that he came into conflict with the municipal governors over club management on several occasions. Besides, Wanda's repeated victories contributed to the football fans' ever-rising expectations. The pressure from Dalian city government, along with widespread illegal gambling and corruption in the football world, gradually planted the seeds of Wang Jianlin's retreat from football.

In the Chinese FA Cup semi-final on 27 September 1998, Dalian Wanda FC took on Liaoning FC. Wang Jianlin was dissatisfied with the referee's decision for three penalty shots and thereafter announced his "perpetual retreat from the football world". This was the catalyst for Wanda's complete withdrawal from football. Further disillusioned by the gambling and corruption revealed in the Chinese football world in 2000, the Wanda brand completed the final step in its divorce from football and Dalian Wanda FC became a thing of the past.

After retreating from football, Wang Jianlin focused all his energy on running Wanda Group. Soon after, Wanda Plazas were gradually starting to be constructed all over the country. Nonetheless, Wang Jianlin's heart was still devoted to football. He mentioned the possibility of returning to football in one of his speeches at Fudan University. He said: "In considering whether or not to return to football, we must first understand why we retreated from football in the first place. There are two reasons for that. Firstly, it was because of the helplessness I felt at the current system. In its current form, football is run by officials. All I do is provide money, but I have no say in the management of the club. For me, there is no excitement in that. When Wanda came onto the scene, nothing changed. Are you asking me when will I come back? When official-governed football is turned into market-governed football, I will be sure to return and when I return, we will be the best."

RETURN TO FOOTBALL

On 3 July 2011, the chairman of the board of Dalian Wanda Group, Wang Jianlin, who had once resolutely stated that he was leaving the world of Chinese football behind, announced that he was returning to the football world after an interval of more than ten years. The difference was that this time he did not intend to finance any single club. Wanda's plan was as follows: during the following three years, Wanda was going to provide at least ¥500 million of capital. The aim was to work out strategic cooperation with the Chinese Football Association. The key points included the sponsorship of the Chinese Super League and support for youth football.

As early as January 2011, Liu Yandong, the then State Councillor, presided over a conference aimed at revitalizing Chinese football. The theme of this conference was that "the central government takes great interest in the reform and development of football." Wang Jianlin at once announced that as long as Chinese football had the need for it, Wanda was ready to support it fully. Investments of several hundred million yuan were possible.

This verbal promise was fulfilled half a year later. A conference for signing a contract of strategic cooperation between the Chinese Football Association and Dalian Wanda Group took place at the Beijing Institute of Technology on 3 July. According to the contract, Dalian Wanda Group was to provide a minimum of ¥500 million over the period of three years to actively support the revitalization of Chinese football. At the same time, a Wanda-sponsored project for sending rising Chinese footballers to study in Europe was officially launched. The value of individual sponsorship was a record high in the history of professional leagues, or even in the history of Chinese sport in general.

When the event came to an end, Liu Yandong shook Wang Jianlin's hand, saying: "You did a good thing. It is even more important now that Chinese football is at its lowest." Wang Jianlin had no plan of relying on his sponsorship of football to directly bring in revenue. He had a more long-term plan.

"There is no place for earning money here, nor can we say that this project is a task delegated to us by the government. If we don't do it, no one will force us into it." For Wang Jianlin the primary requirement was to establish ground for working together and he was willing to accept a tacit understanding on both parts. Wang Jianlin maintained that the reason why he was once more able to bring himself to invest in Chinese football after his disheartened departure was because of the confidence he had in the anti-corruption and anti-gambling movement in the football world in 2009.

Wang Jianlin said: "If we wish to cleanse the football world, we must at the very least ensure that the top levels retain a tough stance. The reason why I am willing to make a comeback is because I learned that from now on the Ministry of Public Security will be present at all Chinese Super League matches, as well as at other national competitions. As senior directors have promised, a 'tough stance' will be maintained throughout."

Wanda's ¥500 million contract over three years was binding in six different areas:

1. Wanda was to be the title sponsor for the Chinese Super League.

2. The group was to introduce development programmes for under-16s and give promising young players the opportunity to pursue further study with top European football clubs.

3. Wanda would contribute funds and time to the Chinese Youth League and strive to expand it.

4. Wanda would not hesitate to employ top foreign coaches in the role of head coach, regardless of the cost.

5. Referee checks and the referee reward system were to be strengthened.

6. The development of the Chinese female national football team was to be strongly supported.

With money in their hands, the Chinese Football Association set out on an impressive headhunt. Soon afterwards, the former Spanish football star José Antonio Camacho was hired as a coach for the Chinese national team. It did not take long for Wang Jianlin to realize that his money was not being spent wisely.

The Football Association signed a three-and-a-half-year contract with Camacho. According to the contract, Camacho's coaching team was promised a yearly salary of €4.3 million after tax deductions. This was among the top ten highest salaries in the football world. However, the contract stipulated no rigid rules or assessment criteria regarding the team's performance. In other words, the Chinese Football Association had no right to unilaterally terminate the contract.

Everyone was hoping that the Spanish football star would be able to lead the Chinese national team on to the 2014 World Cup in Brazil. How disappointed they were when the Chinese national team did not even get into the top 10.

With no visible turnaround in the national team and a failure to qualify for the Asian Cup, public opinion heavily leaned in favour of Camacho 'ending the show'. However, the bilateral contract did not include any restrictive measures, so Camacho pocketed his high salary as agreed and continued to fulfil the role of head coach of the national team. It was only on 15 June 2016, when the Chinese national team suffered a crushing 1–5 defeat to Thailand, that the Chinese Football Association, faced with Chinese football fans' unbearable rage, finally made up its mind and forced Camacho to stand down.

The main reason the Chinese Football Association was so hesitant in making Camacho step down was money. Because the Chinese had unilaterally terminated the contract,

Camacho, under the terms of the contract, requested tremendously high compensation. Wanda Group, having already made a loss on the money previously paid, refused to pay the penalty for the breach of contract. This put the Football Association in an extremely awkward situation. The association also became a target of public criticism for having signed an ill-drafted contract in the first place. In the end, Camacho and the Chinese Football Association agreed to terminate the contract, but the value of the compensation was kept secret.

In July 2014, the central government set up special inspection teams. The Football Association Centre just happened to be on the list of organizations to be inspected in the first round. Before the start of the first inspections, Wang Qishan, the central figure in the anti-corruption campaign, presided over a mobilization meeting. As the team leader, he clearly stated: "Inspections shall be carried out wherever there is trouble."

Camacho's contract was to be included in the upcoming round of audits. Wanda may have hoped to find out what had happened to its investment. Wang Jianlin, who had ample experience with large investments, knew that money had the power to improve a team's performance in the short term, but it could not save Chinese football. "The key problem in Chinese football is the design and reform of the system." He admitted that he himself was "just a sponsor, no more than a large wallet".

Having once given inspiring team talks in the changing rooms, Wang Jianlin no longer insisted on having control over a football team of his own. He concentrated instead on paving the way for freedom of speech at the highest levels of the system.

THE FUTURE OF CHINESE FOOTBALL

Wang Jianlin admitted that his decision to leave Chinese football was made in a fit of anger. Although he swore never to come anywhere near football again, he was unable to let go of his fondness for the sport. Football was his dream. In his opinion, the reason the Chinese team never made it out of Asia was that the basic pool of footballers in China was not strong enough. This was quite clear from the number of youth players: according to incomplete statistics, currently there are only about 10,000 young footballers in China. When compared to neighbouring Asian countries Japan and South Korea, the difference is staggering. Both Japan and South Korea have over 100,000 young footballers.

Simply looking at the situation from this perspective, Wang Jianlin could clearly see the discrepancy. The decisive element in developing a sport is whether or not the sport can be popularized at a local level. For example, the reason table tennis became the Chinese national sport is that one can find table tennis tables almost anywhere around the country. The enthusiasm with which people have thrown themselves into the sport has facilitated China's domination of table tennis championships over the past couple of years.

This is why Wang Jianlin focused his efforts on youth development. He did not set his hopes on changing the Chinese football scene immediately; rather he hoped to see a real rise in Chinese football over the next eight to ten years.

Apart from this, Wang Jianlin also funded the Chinese female national football team because he believed that for sport performance to improve it had to be developed on all sides. Only then could the competitive level increase. Although women's football was not as popular as men's football, the female teams qualified in competitions more often than the male teams. In this instance, Wang Jianlin's reason for funding the Chinese female national team was primarily to lift the team's morale. He not only funded coaches for the team, he also sponsored the Chinese Female Super League.

Wang Jianlin's vision for Chinese football was similar to that of other entrepreneurs who had managed football clubs. Their opinion was that if Chinese football wanted to step onto a path of healthy development, it first had to shed its current form of official control. Only then could Chinese football fully integrate with the market and become a kind of enterprise.

In other words, if Chinese football did not shake off the hand of officialdom, it would struggle to develop in any meaningful way and could even stumble into a dead end. However, reform is always a slow process. It had only been a few decades since the foundation of the Chinese Football Association. In those years the People's Republic of China had only just come into being. There were a thousand things waiting to be done. The Chinese economy was backward, not to speak of the state that football development was in. This was a relic of the era when many companies were nationalized. Now, with the rapid development of the Chinese economy as well as the constant advance towards an integrated global economy, systemic reform had also arrived in China. But many government agencies saw the reforms delayed since they touched upon the interests of multiple stakeholders. The Chinese Football Association was one such example.

Due to football's high profile and popularity, many private entrepreneurs had their eyes on a large slice of this cake. From the early days they used all kinds of rewards to motivate players to win important matches. Later on, entrepreneurs used football as a sports business card helping them to tap into new markets.

Wang Jianlin's opinion of the overall direction of Chinese football's development was that it hinged on private capital. The intervention of private capital was like splashing oil in a boiling hot pot of noodles. As well as having the effect of stimulating the players' zeal on the pitch, it also served to raise the audience's enthusiasm and breathe life into Chinese football. After all, football was one of the first sports in the world to be played competitively.

When Wang Jianlin left the football world, there was no visible change. On the contrary, corruption became ever more evident. At that time, a number of club managers, including the Chairman of Shide who took over Dalian Wanda FC, joined forces in calling for a reform of the football system, but without success.

The general opinion of private enterprises in the football business, together with frequent scandals involving football officials, worsened the Chinese Football Association's already precarious situation. It could be only a matter of time until it stumbled.

Wang Jianlin believed that the current situation was, at first sight, unfavourable for the development of football. Looking at it from a more long-term perspective, however, Chinese football might yet benefit from this situation – the organization crumbled from the top down, which not only had an effect on the development of the football industry, but more importantly facilitated the sport's march towards industrialization. This in turn might help the football industry to shed the shackles of officialism sooner and bring about full-scale commercialization.

If he really wanted to radically change the current situation in Chinese football, he would have to 'marry' it to the market from within. Only then could Chinese football thrive under the market's operating mechanism. In other words, Chinese football can only climb out of the abyss onto a path of healthy development if it manages to conduct a thorough reform.

In 2015, Wanda bought a 20% share in Atlético Madrid, the winner of La Liga that year, for €45 million. On 18 March 2016, FIFA signed a 15-year-long strategic cooperation contract with Wanda. Wanda became FIFA's first major Chinese sponsor.

In its role as FIFA partner, Wanda Group plans to play a greater role in bids for the World Cup and other large-scale international competitions. Wanda also hopes to bring Chinese football on a par with the rest of international football, as well as increasing China's influence on the international football scene. Although the level of Chinese football is comparatively low, the support of one of the world's most powerful sponsors will help it to benefit from international football expertise. With Wanda's help, Chinese football will become more professional, more commercial and increasingly revitalized. Each step that Wang Jianlin has taken in this field has led him closer to fulfilling his promise of breathing life back into Chinese football.

CHAPTER

4

BUILDING A FOUNDATION FOR THE WORLD

ON TOP OF THE WORLD

With increasing experience, Wanda reached new heights, be it in commercial real estate, the cinema industry or in the football world. With its constantly upgraded products and ever-growing lines of business, Wanda's horizons have also widened accordingly. No longer satisfied with countrywide development, Wang Jianlin cast his sights further afield with plans for international development.

Wang Jianlin had always hoped that Wanda would turn into a world-class enterprise and become one of *Fortune* magazine's Global 500 corporations. He wanted the Wanda brand to make its voice heard on the world stage and win honour for Chinese enterprises. Wang Jianlin's patriotism was completely intertwined with his commercial ambition.

Wang Jianlin summarized this point in an address to the media: "I feel a sense of duty. In my eyes, the Oriental Movie Metropolis project is not only Wanda's dream, it also shoulders the heavy responsibility of establishing a Chinese cultural world brand. This is the aim of my work in the cultural industry. I also strive to turn appropriate concepts into Chinese cultural symbols with global significance. As you can see, it is not all about Wanda's reputation or business transformation. There is a definite element of social responsibility in it as well."

As early as 18 December 2011, Wanda Group signed an agreement with three Spanish football clubs, Atlético Madrid, Valencia CF and Villarreal CF, which detailed an overseas training plan for rising Chinese stars. Wanda invested ¥200 million into this programme. The responsibility for overseeing the training programme was given to Shi Xueqing, who had just recently vacated the post of general manager for the cultural department in the Dalian Wanda Group. Wang Jianlin's large investments attracted speculation from the outside world. The majority agreed that Spain was going to be Wanda's first choice for showcasing itself to the world.

In 2012, Wang Jianlin spoke about Wanda's latest developments in the cultural sphere at two press conferences, revealing his plans for launching Wanda's international expansion. When he later made a speech at Tsinghua University in April of the same year, he was even clearer about his plans: "During the following year, Wanda shall predominantly focus on transnational operations. The world will stand witness to an astonishing acquisition."

In 2012, Dalian Wanda Group signed a strategic cooperation contract with the Export–Import Bank of China. The latter agreed to support Dalian Wanda Group in the travel and culture industry as well as in the matter of transnational acquisition operations.

On the afternoon of 21 May 2012, an exceptionally exciting day for Dalian Wanda employees, Wang Jianlin committed US$3.1 billion and signed an acquisition agreement with AMC Entertainment Holdings. From that day on, Wang Jianlin became a shareholder of this US company, the second-largest cinema chain in the world. The event generated wide interest. The sensitive topic of Chinese businesses' acquisition of transnational companies once more instigated controversy.

The central point of the controversy was that Wang Jianlin's act was perhaps yet another example of "the Chinese paying American debts". Several years prior to this, the head of computer manufacturer Lenovo, Liu Chuanzhi, had taken a similar course of action by acquiring IBM's ThinkPad division. When Wang Jianlin followed in Liu's footsteps, many people asked themselves what the practical purpose of transnational acquisition was. How much money would Chinese entrepreneurs have to spend before they finally understood the truth of the large fish devouring the small ones?

Wang Jianlin offered the following response: "From the perspective of Chinese businesses, it was quite natural to commit a considerable sum of money if one hoped to achieve real transnational acquisition. It depends on what you call a considerable sum of money, because regardless of which country a business is from, they all dream of becoming global corporations. Influence only comes with scale-enlargement. Only then can a business hope to be at the very top of the industry and only then will their voice count."

The way that Wang Jianlin saw it, Wanda's acquisition of AMC Theatres was not a question of cost. It was a question of whether or not a Chinese enterprise can truly take on the world. The strategic insight of Chinese entrepreneurs was also an important element in the decision-making process. To put it another way, from the point of view of an entrepreneur, acquisitions are only measured by their potential for profit. This, without exception, holds true equally for both national and transnational acquisitions.

AMC Theatres had a total of 346 cinemas worldwide. It was the largest 3D screen operator in the world. It was clear that the hundred or so cinemas in downtown areas in North America had been selected for their strategic location. This gave the chain a competitive advantage that cinemas in other locations could not match. Through this transnational acquisition Wanda, in one move, became the world's largest cinema operator. By then, Wanda owned 428 cinemas and controlled 5,758 screens. However, Wang Jianlin was still not satisfied. He announced that Wanda was constantly going to align itself with the market and complete comprehensive transnational development.

At the time of Wanda's acquisition of AMC Theatres, many on the outside referred to the event as 'an ant devouring an elephant'. In Wang Jianlin's opinion, however, AMC Theatres was no elephant and Wanda was not an ant, rather a colony of ants. After a lengthy two-year negotiation process, they finally arrived at the acquisition plan, ready to put on an 'ant devouring an elephant' show that would command the world's attention.

Looking at the situation from an objective economic development point of view, a good number of economists agreed with Wang Jianlin that the "ant devouring an elephant" phenomenon was not uncommon in the commercial world. However, Wanda's acquisition of AMC Theatres took place between two different countries: one was the US, the richest country in the world, and the other was rapidly developing China. What drew the attention of people from over the world was the fact that the 'ant' was Chinese and the 'elephant' was American.

Wang Jianlin commented that if it had been an American enterprise that had acquired a Chinese one, people would not have been so surprised. But the way he saw it, it didn't matter which nation's enterprise got acquired by another nation's enterprise. It all fell under accepted business practice.

At the beginning of 2016, Wanda Group announced that it had purchased the majority of Legendary Entertainment's shares for no more than US$3.5 billion. This has, up until now, been the largest cross-border mergers and acquisitions (M&A) operation carried out by a Chinese enterprise in the culture industry. Wang Jianlin stated during the contract-signing ceremony that through this move he wanted to amplify Dalian Wanda Group's voice in the film industry. "Wanda already enjoys great influence in the Chinese film industry, but that is far from enough. The film market is global, which is why we must win influence. Currently, a couple of large American companies control the global film market. How do we effect change? By relying on Wanda's step-by-step approach."

BUILDING A 'CULTURAL CARRIER'

When the AMC Theatres acquisition case was settled, the global audience increasingly started paying more attention to Wanda's activities on the cultural scene. Many people no longer associated Wang Jianlin primarily with commercial real estate. They started to see him and get to know him in a completely new light. This also contributed to his growing 'cultural ambitions'.

Wang Jianlin's ambitions in commercial real estate were widely known. In the cultural sphere, however, he put together an astonishing team of people in just eight years – the Wanda Culture Industry Group. It originally served as Wanda's back-up force, but after eight years of hard struggle the company evolved into a dominant force that would be hard to overlook in the Chinese culture sphere.

In the course of a mere eight years, the Wanda Culture Industry Group was commanding the attention of the whole world. Although it had the might of Wanda and Wang Jianlin watching its back, the group certainly did not have an easy ride.

Wang Jianlin once explained that he was not, after all, an artist. He was a businessman. What businessmen need to consider is how to expand the business and how to establish a transnational business brand. As for the long-term development aims of the Wanda Culture Industry Group, it was perfectly possible for it to promote national culture as well.

One of the business lines in commercial real estate for Wanda Group is the Wanda Hotels. Wanda Group has already constructed 32 Wanda Hotels in cooperation with the world's top five hotel management companies. In Wanda Hotel management, Wang Jianlin maintained the following strategy throughout: Step out, bring in, open up.

Only after having 'stepped out' into the world can one discover one's weaknesses. As a result of that one can "bring in" modern management concepts from abroad. In the last step, one can finally fully implement the "opening up" of the business on the global market.

With ample experience in hotel management under Wanda's belt, Wanda Culture Industry Group only had to 'step out' along the road already trodden. Similarly, Wanda's acquisition of AMC Theatres laid a strong foundation for the transnational expansion of Wanda Hotels.

Wang Jianlin had plenty of experience in guiding Wanda through the 'stepping out' phase. In the eyes of the outside world, Wanda was brimming with ambition. This was true, but it was certainly not the whole story. As the captain of this cultural carrier, Wang Jianlin was more than capable of steering his ship out of the Asian harbour and successfully making landfall across the ocean.

Wanda's two decades of development, be it in terms of its ever-broadening scale or the rapid increase of Wanda's output, astonished a good number of entrepreneurs. Wang Jianlin's greatest insight during this period was the importance of constant innovation in the industry's operating model. Under his leadership, Wanda adopted an operating model similar to that of a transnational enterprise. It would not take long for Wanda to set sail and cast off, ploughing the ocean waves.

THE DREAM OF A 'CHINESE HOLLYWOOD'

In total, Wanda had only been active in the cultural industry for eight years. During these years, Wang Jianlin had climbed to the very top of the Chinese cinema business, achieving unequalled hegemony in Asia. With the acquisition of AMC Theatres, Wanda's scale and power moved to a whole new level. It truly became worthy of being called the industry leader.

AMC Theatres had been making a loss in the three years prior to being acquired by Wanda in 2012. The following year, AMC Theatres made a profit. It was a shocking revelation for many. For the majority of foreign entrepreneurs, Wanda was just a little-known Chinese enterprise. How, then, could it possess the ability to turn around the state of AMC Theatres?

During the launch ceremony for the Oriental Movie Metropolis in Qingdao in September 2013, the media touched on the topic of AMC Theatres. Wang Jianlin avoided the question and steered the topic of discussion away. Instead, he spoke with confidence about the film and television industry park that was to start operating in Qingdao. He pointed out that neither in China nor elsewhere had there been an equivalent of the Oriental Movie Metropolis project, both in terms of its scale and the amount of money that was invested in it.

The construction of the whole project took up an area of 3.76 million square metres. The floor area came to 5.4 million square metres. Moreover, the Oriental Movie Metropolis was not limited to film and television production. There was also a museum, an exhibition centre, a film-star wax-works museum and other film- and television-related projects. Other facilities included the Wanda travel and culture city, resort hotels, a yacht club, live *Top Gear* shows and a whole street of seaside bars.

Wang Jianlin explained that in the Qingdao project Wanda was going to put all its efforts into constructing the largest film and television base and resort city in the world; here Wang Jianlin's long-term dream was laid out for all to see.

Wanda's investment in the whole project exceeded ¥5 billion. Such a large sum naturally attracted a high level of attention from overseas. A number of foreign media channels joined in the excitement generated by the project, not to mention the Chinese media who feverishly competed to report on the event. The world-renowned financial newspaper, the *Wall Street Journal*, even conducted an interview with Wang Jianlin. He revealed during the launch ceremony that the reason Wanda was willing to invest such a large sum of money was that they wanted to build a 'Chinese Hollywood'.

Many people did not hide their scepticism at Wang Jianlin's ambitious dream. Although Wanda possessed abundant financial resources and Wang Jianlin himself did not lack courage, there was no way of knowing whether the world's first Oriental Movie Metropolis had any chance of matching the prestigious Hollywood.

Wang Jianlin was quite clear that there were inevitable differences between Eastern and Western culture. Even if these differences became less conspicuous as a result of the process of economic and cultural globalization, they nonetheless still existed. These cultural differences caused East Asian concepts of film and television to differ from Western ones. Despite China having a rich cultural heritage, including a good number of excellent literary works, it was not until 2012 that the Nobel Prize for Literature was awarded to a Chinese writer.

Impressions of Chinese culture are limited in the West. The reason behind the launching of the Oriental Movie Metropolis was to market Chinese culture. The emphasis, however, was on how China, along with other East Asian countries, should showcase its local culture to the West.

Such thinking explains why Wang Jianlin acquired AMC Theatres. He now had plenty of room for showcasing China's, as well as other East Asian countries', outstanding cultural works. Wang Jianlin felt that only under such conditions could he achieve a real cultural exchange between Eastern and Western countries.

Using AMC Theatres as a platform to promptly promote Chinese films, such as *Lost in Thailand*, on the international market was very successful and, as a result, Wang Jianlin's plan for the future of the Oriental Movie Metropolis became ever clearer in his mind. Through repeated trial and error, Wang Jianlin discovered that although there were undeniable differences between Westerners' and Asians' habits, when it came to art, culture knew no borders.

In his youth, Wang Jianlin once read some poems by the English Poet Laureate, William Wordsworth, and found that the imagery used was no different from that used by Chinese poets. For this reason, Wang Jianlin believed that the way to make Asian culture accepted in the West was not to change Asia's rich cultural heritage by adjusting it to Western norms, but to make Westerners really understand Asian culture.

What people saw when they looked at the Qingdao project was a magnificent feat accomplished by Wanda's rising star – the culture industry group. It can also be said that it was another innovation in Wanda's process of enterprise transformation. Concealed behind the Qingdao Oriental Movie Metropolis was Wanda's huge commercial empire, governed by the Wanda way.

In 2012, Wanda Group officially established a film production company and started to show its talents in the film production business. The romantic comedy *Holding Love* was a big hit on Chinese Valentine's Day, thanks to the good timing of the film schedule and enthusiastic support from cinemas. Wanda Media Co. Ltd. announced that it would be investing in at least eight films per year, starting from 2013. Among the films Wanda invested in were crime thriller *Police Story 2013*, martial arts drama *Man of Tai Chi* and historical romance *The Palace*. The Wanda-sponsored historical drama *Coming Home,* released in March 2014, was well received both by audiences and critics.

Wanda Media's 2014 film plan included masterpieces such as *The Great Hypnotist,* scheduled for the May Day holiday, and the adventure fantasy thriller *Mojin: The Lost Legend.* Other films spanned several different genres, from thrillers to romances.

However, Chinese film production was still facing a number of obstacles, chiefly an insufficient talent pool in the industry, limits on technology, and film censorship. The result was that the Chinese film industry remained small and cinema chains continued to rely largely on imported films. As for whether Wang Jianlin's dream of a Chinese Hollywood can come true, this still remains to be seen.

BUILDING A CULTURAL CITY OF TOURISM

Another of Wanda's wins on its path to transnational expansion was the acquisition of British yacht builder Sunseeker International and the establishment of a real estate development company in the UK. At the start of 2014, Wanda made plans to invest £2-3 billion in an urban development construction project in Britain and to purchase Madrid's iconic building, the Edificio España, for the massive sum of €265 million.

Sunseeker International had a history dating back to 1968. Having been in operation for several decades, it had early on become one of the world's top brands in luxury motor yacht manufacturing. It was also the British royal family's favoured yacht brand. The company had over 2,500 employees and a strong market position, with an annual turnover as high as US$5 million. Wang Jianlin was filled with confidence by this move. He maintained that yachts, as the flagship product of high-end luxury goods, would dominate millionaires' consumption trends.

Originally, in accordance with its established strategy, Wanda had intended to set up yacht clubs in Dalian, Qingdao and Sanya. Each was to be provided with at least 10 yachts as well as 300 moorings in order to attract other yachts. After careful consideration, though, Wang Jianlin came to the conclusion that, rather than buying 30 yachts, it was better to buy a yacht manufacturing company, so in the end Wanda decided to go for Sunseeker.

During the process of expansion, Wang Jianlin's strategy was not only to minimize interference in the management style of each company but also to take full advantage of the existing management staff by stimulating their initiative. Following the acquisition of Sunseeker, he did not send a single Wanda employee there. Wang Jianlin said: "Our acquisition of the company is nothing more than having a new general manager. With appropriate policies in place, we trust that Sunseeker employees will do an even better job."

With regard to transnational M&A, Wanda has always adhered to three criteria:

1. Wanda aims to invest in and conduct M&A operations in countries with flourishing economies and mature markets.

2. "M&A operations are primary; investment is secondary."

3. Companies chosen for M&A operations must deal with industries that are already closely related to Wanda's. The primary focus is to be on culture, tourism and retail.

Wanda spent heavily on purchasing the yacht business in order to stimulate diversified development as well as development in the tourism sector. When Wanda contracted the building of a large-scale tourist resort, Wang Jianlin made an important discovery. He believed that the decisive point between success and failure with these kinds of projects was whether or not Wanda could achieve a rational transfer of resources across the world.

The building of a cultural tourism city was Wang Jianlin's attempt at rational transfer of the resources that were available to him. In Wang Jianlin's vision, the Yangtze River Delta held an especially important position and therefore required exceptional attention. Wang Jianlin had previously led a group to scout out the locations of Ningbo, Nanjing and Wuxi. After rigorous analysis, in the end they settled on Wuxi. Wuxi is located in the middle of a triangle formed by

Shanghai, Nanjing and Hangzhou. Its geographical advantage was evident.

After careful planning, Wanda Cultural Tourism City was set to be built in the Binhu district of Wuxi city. The total area spanned 2.02 million square metres, with floor space covering 3.4 million square metres. Wanda's investment in the project equalled ¥21 billion. It was split across four sectors: culture, tourism, commerce and hotels. It included Wanda City, a large-scale stage show, a large theme park and resort hotels.

Wang Jianlin said: "I have exerted the most effort on this project, I have spent the longest amount of time on planning it and the number of innovations is also the greatest." For example, water parks are common enough, but Wanda was committed to building a "fourth generation" water park. Much of the equipment was custom-made and unique. "We have put a lot of research into this programme. An international team of experts took care of the design, incorporating Wuxi's local cultural story as well as interactive exhibitions."

Wang Jianlin claimed during a media interview that he had previously scouted Wuxi on many occasions. The design team also went back and forth countless times, racking their brains for over half a year on how best to let the culture element of the project express Wuxi's local culture. In the end, they designed an outdoor theme park with six distinct sections. Each section strove to exhibit a local speciality. For example, the well-renowned purple clay pottery played an important part in the exhibition.

What kind of culture industry was suited to China? This was a question that Wang Jianlin believed needed special consideration. The origins and development of Chinese traditional culture, as well as the specialities of Wuxi's local culture, were all elements that Wang Jianlin hoped to communicate to society through the Wuxi Wanda City. This involved a process of sifting through mythology, local culture, traditional crafts and other key concepts.

When Wang Jianlin was building the Wuxi Wanda Cultural Tourism City, he wished it to be a further step along the road out of China and onto the world stage. The aim was to build a Chinese culture brand.

Wang Jianlin said: "With the end of large-scale development in Chinese real estate, it is highly unlikely that we could achieve sustainable development of both the tourist and real estate industries. My guess is that we might be able to retain it for a maximum of eight to ten years. Luckily, within eight to ten years the cultural tourism scene will have fully developed." In Wang Jianlin's opinion it was an inherent advantage that the Wuxi Wanda City was built on native soil.

"With a history of 5,000 years or so, the vitality encased within Chinese culture is self-evident. Wanda wants to reactivate traditionally Chinese culture and values through exposing Chinese consumers to a taste for brands. When the time comes, these values will be brought out to the world." In this respect, it seemed, Wang Jianlin had no fear of being a daring forerunner.

CHAPTER

5

A THOUGHT OF A CENTURY LASTS FOR A CENTURY

ENTERPRISE CULTURE

After 30 years of growth, Dalian Wanda had been transformed from a small, little-known company into a large-scale enterprise that combined five different industries – culture, commercial real estate, chain department stores, tourism investment and high-class hotels – in one enterprise. The speed of Wanda's development was astonishing, and the reason Wanda grew at such a pace was closely linked to Wang Jianlin's management skills.

Wang Jianlin paid close attention to maintaining a human approach in the process of enterprise management. In building his business, he retained a people-centred approach from the onset. Only by exerting great effort in caring for its employees was Wanda able to attract international talent. More specifically, the care Wang Jianlin expended on his employees mainly manifested itself in the following ways.

First, the standard salary Wanda offered to its employees was the highest in all of China for the industry. Wanda practised a seniority wage system among its grass-roots employees – all Wanda employees got a ¥1,200 bonus for each year of service, on top of their regular income. After five years, the seniority bonus alone equalled ¥6,000, which was unheard-of in any other enterprise within the industry. Wanda's employees felt grateful for the generous treatment, and so were willing to exert the utmost effort to do their bit for the company. It is safe to say that this played an important role in helping Wanda Group grow at such a fast pace.

Secondly, as well as generous remuneration, Wanda set up a comprehensive training system for employees. Every year, the group spent hundreds of millions of yuan on training. It also invested ¥700 million in building their employees a 12-hectare Wanda College in Langfang city, Hebei province.

The college floor space covered over 120,000 square metres and it could accommodate more than 3,000 people. It consisted of an administrative building, teaching buildings, outdoor sports ground, indoor gym, dormitories, enterprise exhibition hall and a canteen. Teaching was carried out using the most advanced equipment available in China, supported by exceptional infrastructure. It counted among the top business schools in China.

Since the building of Wanda College, Wanda Group has arranged for the company's middle and high-level managers to attend training at the college on a yearly basis. The college has nurtured countless outstanding managers, building a strong base for Wanda's rapid development.

Thirdly, Wanda Group took extra care to treat its employees well from day to day. Wang Jianlin required that there be a company canteen. No distinction was made between headquarters and branch companies: all Wanda employees were provided with free meals during the working day. Apart from this, Wanda practised an internal 'happy holiday' system. Employees who were judged to be outstanding could take advantage of this. They not only had the freedom to choose a destination out of all Wanda hotels in the country, they were also reimbursed for a return flight ticket as well as for accommodation. They could even get flight and accommodation costs reimbursed for two other relatives. Such generous treatment greatly improved the employees' satisfaction level. They worked even harder to be judged as outstanding employees, which gradually increased the efficiency of the business.

Wanda's management approach not only made employees feel valued, but also contributed to increasing the employee retention rate. Compared to other businesses in the industry, Wanda's employee turnover was the lowest.

Most of the world's top businesses emphasize employee care in their company culture. For that reason, if Wanda wished to become a top-level company, it had to adopt a people-centred approach.

Wang Jianlin's thoughts regarding this matter can be summarized in the following way.

First, at its most fundamental, a company is a social institution. It is not a simple tool used by people to chase after profits, as portrayed in theoretical or "blackboard" economics. Companies satisfy people's need for coexisting with others in mutual trust and jointly striving for a purpose. An enterprise brings people together and allows them to maximize the productive forces within society. At the same time, it makes people undertake duties and responsibilities that come with coexisting with one's environment. People are constantly influenced by new information, thoughts and beliefs. When a company lacks an environment which helps people to stretch their abilities and encourages them in mutual communication and understanding, then its employees will naturally take no active part in contributing.

Secondly, employees should be a bridge for connecting the company with clients and with society. Creating client value is the basis for the survival and growth of any enterprise. How, then, should an enterprise find out and cater to clients' needs? By relying on grass-roots employees.

The basis of enterprise development and expansion is reliant on the work efficiency of grass-roots employees. If a company does not practise a people-centred approach and does not take good care of its employees, then the link between employees, clients and society will be broken. The resulting situation is unfavourable for the long-term development of the company.

This is why a company should set up a people-centred approach by taking good care of all its employees. Only then can the company's employees do their utmost for the growth of the business by connecting the company with its own clients and with society at large.

Thirdly, the company should strive to unleash the creativity of its employees. Within the current concept of modern management, the creativity (or lack thereof) of a company's employees is an important determinant of whether or not the business can sustain growth. Only when a company does not focus solely on profit, but also remembers to treat its employees humanely, can it hope to fully unleash the employees' creativity, and in so doing maximize the company's value.

If the employees work in a hostile environment full of envy and petty scheming, where would they find the energy for being creative? This is why a company should provide its employees with a comfortable environment. In this way, the employees will be able to feel relaxed while at the same time automatically improving the company's core values.

Wanda's people-centred approach – the provision of an excellent working environment, the system of positive encouragement and the generous treatment of its employees – all helped to attract talent on an even bigger scale. It provided a never-ending pool of resources for driving the company's development.

THE WAY TO INNOVATION

One of the overriding themes of Wanda Group's course of development is the shining glory of "innovation". It is safe to say that innovation played an irreplaceable role in bringing about Wanda's successes. Wang Jianlin valued the company's ability to innovate. He once said to the media: "In my opinion, the company's profitability and innovation ability are our core competitive advantages."

Wanda Group put a high value on innovation from the start, in its business model, marketing, thought and management style. This is how Wanda was able to pioneer countless "firsts" in the real estate industry.

In 1989, Wanda made itself heard in what was then a very chaotic real estate market by breaking through the limit on the standard surface area of a flat. This was a first in the real estate market. Naturally, it roused exclamations of astonishment from the public. Furthermore, Wanda Group also introduced novel concepts in interior design, such as bathrooms and hallways with windows, which left an even deeper impression on the public.

Three years later, Wanda led the way in introducing European-style mansions and residences. This innovative move then set off a European-style trend in the real estate market.

Looking back over Wanda's numerous innovative moves, the most representative of them all must be the group's contract model. This model has prevailed since 2001 and its success has been astonishing. Wanda's contract real estate model allowed it to get ahead of its competitors, while at the same generating considerable profit.

Many experts have agreed that this kind of commercial model could not be replicated. Each time Wanda imported its model into a new city, the location it chose was bound to become the city's busiest place. It propelled the city's economic development and tax revenue. It was widely believed that no other company could achieve this. No company but Wanda could attract both Chinese and foreign business and create a frenzied scuffle to secure a spot in the Wanda Plaza. Equally, no other business could enter a new city and secure rent contracts before building a shopping mall, as Wanda did so as to guarantee the launch of a fully operational, bustling plaza.

Wanda's innovative commercial model was highly praised by the Chinese government. It was also loudly praised on the international scene. Undoubtedly, this commercial model was a success. What, then, led to this commercial model being adopted by Wanda?

First, this approach was required in order to realize Wanda's business concept of becoming an enterprise spanning a century.

Wanda's corporate philosophy today centres on: "Wanda International, an enterprise spanning a century". In order to fulfil this ambition, there must be a stable material base as well as an enterprise culture. As for an enterprise culture, Wanda already has one. Simply speaking, a stable material base means long-term stable cash flow. Wanda's main aim in constructing shopping centres was precisely to obtain a stable cash flow.

After thorough discussion and analysis, the management of Wanda Group decided to resolve the problem of stable cash flow by leasing commercial properties. In practical terms it meant taking on low-risk but large-scale projects and leasing property to Fortune Global 500 companies. In accordance with this idea, Wanda partnered with Wal-Mart. The first of their joint collaborative programmes was successful, which facilitated Wanda's continued reliance on this model.

Secondly, China's joining of the World Trade Organization required higher standards of Chinese enterprises as a result of the fiercely competitive environment.

There were two main faults with China's traditional retail industry. Firstly, the retail sector was monotonous. With China's entry into the WTO, China opened up its retail industry to the world. The internationally popular one-stop retail business model started to seep into China. This was a major blow for China's traditional retail industry. In view of this, Wanda decided to build one-stop shopping malls, which satisfied both the consumers' demand and the market demand for the retail industry.

The other fault was that the Chinese retail industry preferred a solitary model. Traditional retail industry almost solely consisted of stand-alone businesses, which was not suitable for the developmental path that the Chinese retail industry was to follow later. The main reason why Wal-Mart, Carrefour and similar large enterprises enjoyed high sales as well as consumers' approval was that they pooled their procurements and sold their products at low prices.

In fact, the most popular trend in the global retail industry was the retail chain operating model. An enterprise could only bulk-buy if it had managed to establish this model. Only then could it afford to lower prices and achieve a competitive advantage.

With this in mind, Wanda Group, like the chain stores, satisfied people's demand for basic necessities by building a Wanda Plaza each time it opened up a new destination. These practices made Wanda stand out from its competitors in the real estate sector and gain the public's trust. It was with these considerations in mind that Wanda decided to put into effect the contract real estate commercial model.

The third advantage of the contract real estate model was that it could be governed by transnational business management rules. Most of the largest transnational companies operate on a franchising business model. An example is the well-known American company Yum! Brands, which operates licensed fast-food brands including KFC and Pizza-Hut. The company runs over 1,000 restaurants in China, but only owns one of them.

Wal-Mart, another well-known enterprise, has close to 5,000 stores around the world. The majority of the stores are franchises, less than 20% of stores having their own property rights. We can say that the majority of transnational enterprises, apart from the manufacturing industry, rely on the franchising business model. Upon seeing this trait, Wanda put into effect its contract real estate strategy to attract these transnationals to lease Wanda stores.

Lastly, there was room for expansion in the Chinese market. The population of the US was barely 200 million, yet there were over 10,000 shopping centres. China's population was over 1.3 billion, with room for constructing 20,000 shopping centres. The average salary in China undoubtedly lags behind average US salary, yet it is estimated that by 2020 the average salary in China will reach the current value of Singaporean salary. Looking at it from this point of view, China had great potential for the construction of shopping centres. This was also in accordance with Wanda's enterprise culture and its ambition of becoming 'an enterprise spanning a hundred years'.

Moreover, the contract real estate commercial model was unique in the way it benefited the nation and the people – the Wanda Plazas built by Wanda Group created more job opportunities on the local level while at the same time greatly contributing to local tax revenue.

Besides, whenever Wanda opened up a new city, the multistorey buildings it put up always became symbolic landmarks of each city. This improved the city's image at a business level, which greatly helped the government in inviting investment into the city. Because of this, governments actively supported the building of Wanda Plazas.

It is clear that the innovative contract real estate commercial model complied with market demand and satisfied consumers' requirements for the retail industry. It also greatly contributed to improving the government's performance. More importantly, this commercial model generated a healthy profit for Wanda Group.

There were many more innovative moves in the course of Wanda's development – among others, Wanda was the first enterprise to take on the renovation of crumbling old cities, and the first to practise a cross-regional development strategy. This series of innovative moves enabled Wanda to become a leading Chinese business and at the same time helped to accomplish Wanda's economic miracle.

COMMERCE AND POLITICS

People like to compare the words of those entrepreneurs who stand in the spotlight. The majority of these are Wang Jianlin's friends and peers. Although each of China's richest entrepreneurs has different opinions and a different personal background, they all to some extent interact with politics. Ren Zhiqiang – nicknamed 'Big Gun Ren' when it comes to debating public issues – often comes up with some startling statements during his participation in the administration and discussion of state affairs. During two meetings in 2014 (the National People's Congress and the Chinese People's Political Consultative Conference), he expressed his opinion on housing prices: "China should not levy property tax on private home owners since they do not own the land. The ongoing property tax is not based on land. Instead, rural land and collectively owned land, in fact all land that is profitable, should be taxed."

Another real estate magnate, Pan Shiyi, who often interacts with Ren Zhiqiang on the Weibo microblogging site, is even more of an entrepreneurial star in the public field. His proposals to the government were once criticized as "representing his own interests". During two meetings in Beijing in 2009, Pan Shiyi made three suggestions: "Number one – decrease the rental tax on commercial real estate property; number two – remove the bar on owning more than two houses in Beijing; number three – make the land market more transparent." Some felt that suggestions such as "reducing rental tax on commercial real estate property" or "making the land market more transparent" were more in the interest of his company than the public interest. Pan Shiyi's argument was that first and foremost these recommendations were to safeguard the interests of the individual, and the interests of the industry were only secondary. The unfavourable public perception may have influenced Pan Shiyi's later views. In 2013, he turned his attention to environmental protection. He funded the procurement of devices to monitor the level of PM2.5 (a measure of particles and droplets suspended in the air) and called on the public to pay attention to the environment. He also proposed the introduction of two types of property tax, where people could choose whether they wanted to be taxed based on area or based on the number of properties.

The real estate entrepreneurs who participate in the administration and discussion of state affairs do their best to avoid the topics in which they have a close personal interest.

The dual identity, mixing politics and business, is a double-edged sword. Although in some aspects it might be beneficial to society, in others it might result in overlooking serious threats. Compared to full-time parliamentary members abroad, Chinese entrepreneurial committee members are more effective at inciting a sense of public responsibility and raising queries relating to the interests of the individual.

Wang Jianlin and other real estate magnates are still in the process of trying to figure out where their place is in the limbo between the commercial and the political worlds. Beyond that, with the economic and social transformation taking place, the future may be fraught with risk.

As for the relationship between enterprise and government, Wang Jianlin stated in an interview with the media: "People should not think that we have the same interests or that we are good mates. There is only one reason why Wanda has been able to navigate the political waves, and that is because we always tried to protect ourselves."

Wanda's success is not tied to the government. Instead, it is reliant on Wang Jianlin's correct understanding of politics. In his daily day-to-day management, he pays special attention to the Party's involvement within the company.

As a model example of Party building in a private business, Wanda is often visited by Party officials from government institutions at all levels for the purpose of learning by observation. In recent years, government officials visiting Wanda have included high-ranking officials from the Central Organization Department, leaders from the National Party Committee and the vice-secretary of Liaoning province.

Each time Wanda Group starts a developmental project in a new city, it sets up a Party organization department which is of equal importance to the project department or other key departments. Joining the Party is extremely important within Wanda Group as "Party members have significant advantages over non-Party members, ranging from social benefits to career advancement. This method is rarely seen among private businesses in China."

The attention Wanda attaches to Party building projects is reflected in the annual ceremonies to honour the Party. In 2010, during a major development project in the Changbai Mountains, 58 new Party members gathered by the Yang Jingyu Martyr Cemetery to pledge their vows in honour of the 89th anniversary since the founding of the Party. On 1 July 2011, a Party anniversary, 90 new Party members got a chartered flight to Ji'an city in Jiangxi province to conduct the admission ceremony in the Jinggang Mountains.

Wang Jianlin once remarked that "understanding government policies, following in the Party's footsteps and maintaining good relationships between politics and commerce are the basis for Wanda's development". This statement appropriately reflects Wanda's amicable and harmonious relationship with the government. In addition, Wang Jianlin reads the Party newspapers every day and researches new policy directions.

Wang Jianlin's diligent and smart management won him the government's approval and praise. He was given an audience with state leaders at the National Work Conference on the Development of Private Enterprises on 21 March 2012. The next day Wang Jianlin was one of the few guests invited to take part in the Party building forum and share his experience with Party building in his enterprise. On 10 April of the same year, he received an audience with state leaders as the representative of the winners of the China Charity Awards.

Clearly, by keeping pace with government policy, Wang Jianlin has ensured that Wanda would not err from the right path.

CLOSE TO POLICY, FAR FROM POLITICS

Wanda clearly had a good standing in terms of Party building projects. Wang Jianlin, as a member of the Chinese Communist Party Central Committee (CCPCC), differed from other celebrities or entrepreneurs who only knew how to raise hands in agreement. He showed his individualism to an appropriate degree, using his public reputation to carve out an imperceptible sphere of influence on the limited political scene.

Wang Jianlin directly pointed out during the two sessions in 2012 that the proposal he had submitted the previous year not only did not pass, but was also negligently discarded by the Ministry of Finance. Even today, many of the journalists who attended the two sessions still talk about this.

During the two sessions in 2011, Wang Jianlin submitted a proposal to reduce import tariffs on luxury goods. In order to give more weight to the proposal, he spent over a million yuan on hiring market research firm Nielsen to conduct a survey overseas and collect data on the consumption of luxury goods in China. Wang Jianlin proposed that the State Taxation Administration and the General Administration of Customs, driven by the Ministry of Commerce, jointly introduce a new policy to reduce the import tariff on luxury goods. The idea was that the new policy would attract Chinese luxury consumers, who were becoming more numerous with every passing day, back to China. In doing so, the pace of economic transformation would pick up.

The proposal did not disappear without trace. Wang Jianlin revealed that it gained the agreement and support of some government leaders, but "unfortunately, the proposal failed to be implemented." After the two sessions in 2012, the ministries involved sent a special letter to Wang Jianlin, expressing their gratitude for the attention he was paying to the country's financial matters. Later on, though, they stated: "Import tariffs are not the reason that luxury goods are expensive, since upon calculation, import tariffs on average only make up roughly 2% of the retail price."

"They are trying to fool me," Wang Jianlin said after reading the reply. "I have put great care into preparing this proposal. If we can reduce import tariffs and bring Chinese people's overseas spending back into China, it would be beneficial both for increasing consumption and for creating new jobs."

In order to ensure that each proposal had been carefully read and that each member's suggestions were thoroughly considered, the organization department asked for feedback upon processing each proposal. The choice was between 'satisfied', 'somewhat satisfied', 'dissatisfied' and 'very dissatisfied'. Without hesitation, Wang Jianlin ticked 'very dissatisfied'. In the follow-up to this matter, the Ministry of Finance in the end offered an explanation for the decision, but Wang Jianlin was not at all satisfied with the explanation.

In fact, the quality of recommendations and proposals of CCPCC members as well as the sincerity of administrative bodies' replies and similar confrontations have been hot topics at National People's Congress (NPC) and CCPCC sessions during recent years. Although Wang Jianlin was dissatisfied with the outcome of his proposal, he continued to fulfil his role in the discussion of state affairs with as much enthusiasm as before.

During the two sessions in 2012 where Wang Jianlin 'bombarded' the Ministry of Finance, he also proposed another motion, namely "to restore prime 30% discounted interest rates on loans for first-time home buyers and for first-time house upgrades".

The government's slogan for that year was "to facilitate the return of house prices to a reasonable level". However, Wang Jianlin thought that "even if the national average house price fell by 20%, the common people would not gain any advantages from that." This was because at the same time as the state exercised macroeconomic control of the real estate industry to push prices down, one bank after another responded by abolishing the policy of 30% interest discount on loans for first-time house buyers. Consequently, the house buyers' burden was not lightened at all. On the contrary, for some people buying a house was made even more difficult.

In Wang Jianlin's opinion, of all the parties involved in the macroeconomic adjustment, including the government, real estate industry, house buyers and banks, the only party that walked away laughing was the banks. The other parties gained no benefit from the adjustment.

Wang Jianlin did not directly express his objections to the macroeconomic adjustment of the real estate sector. Instead, under the precondition of showing his approval, he expressed the hope that banks could restore the prime interest rate on house loans. Doing so would stimulate house buying among the middle class. Furthermore, house buyers would see more tangible benefits and the real estate market would be revitalized. It is clear that Wang Jianlin had a sharp perception of the public's intentions and of the government's direction of development.

In view of his status as a member of the Central Committee, Wang Jianlin said that as members of a new social class, private entrepreneurs not only had to perform philanthropic acts, they also had to possess a sense of responsibility towards society. They should take an active part in politics and not underestimate their responsibility to the nation's democracy. This was the duty the new social class should take on.

Apart from his sharp criticism of state organs, Wang Jianlin on many occasions expressed the restraint the economic environment imposed on entrepreneurial spirit. What concerned him most was that in today's China, it was increasingly hard to find an outstanding entrepreneur. Although the commercial world in 1980s China was highly turbulent and the first generation of entrepreneurs advanced warily, they, on the other hand, had no lack of daring commercial ambitions.

He declared: "The greatest problem China is facing today is not whether the economy grows at a slower or faster rate. The greatest problem is the lack of entrepreneurial spirit. At the end of the 80s and beginning of the 90s, many government officials, army officials and professors braved the entrepreneurial ocean, wondering from place to place and doing business in hope of becoming rich. But now, many people do not have the courage. The Chinese entrepreneurial environment, public opinion environment, capital environment and institutional environment are increasingly favourable towards the growth of large companies and do not encourage the development of small entrepreneurs."

At present, increasing numbers of entrepreneurs value enjoyment. They no longer insist on the success and improvement of their businesses. They retire from business as soon as they see some results and abandon the companies that they had once struggled for. This was a frequent cause of sadness to Wang Jianlin, who warned that "if we get to the point where the majority of entrepreneurs no longer have the spirit to fight, when they have all sold their businesses and retired to enjoy life, then our country will be finished."

It was Wang Jianlin's awareness of the situation that drove him to take part in discussions on state affairs, so that he could adjust and push through the relevant policies that might bring about an environment favourable to entrepreneurs. Apart from the formal recommendations passed during official NCP and CCPCC meetings, Wang Jianlin expressed his opinions on people's livelihoods, house prices and similar hot topics in daily life through the media.

Since 2014, the Chinese real estate market has been experiencing a period of downturn, with turnover falling continuously. Some of China's first-tier cities have even witnessed turnover dropping by over 50%. Many have linked the downturn with rumours of the 'collapse' of the real estate market, and real estate magnate Wang Shi predicted that the Chinese market was going to get into a very bad state that year.

Wang Jianlin responded to this mood in February 2015, saying that "the argument for the collapse of the Chinese market is only a continuation of the former argument." He retained his own opinion on the matter throughout. As early as ten years before, there were already those who proclaimed the collapse of the Chinese real estate market. This opinion was echoed by a number of professionals in the field as well as by some renowned economists. Ten years later, however, the Chinese real estate market was still standing.

Wang Jianlin clearly had great confidence in government regulation: "China's level of urbanization has not yet reached 40%. At a work conference on the new type of urbanization at the Third Plenary Session of the Eighteenth CCP Central Committee, urbanization for the first time became one of the central tenets of economic development. It was recognized as a major driving force in stimulating economic development."

In this situation, of course, Wang Jianlin's status was somewhat vague. As a real estate developer himself, it was likely to seem that he was mustering support for the benefit of his own industry. Wang Jianlin's basic strategy for the relationship between politics and commerce was to stay close to the government but keep himself well away from politics.

In his role as a CCPCC member, Wang Jianlin preferred to adopt an active yet non-radical stance in debating public affairs. This was enough to show his willingness to participate in an appropriate manner. In other words, he was able to find the balance between activism and radicalism.

THE FRAGRANCE ALWAYS REMAINS ON THE HAND THAT GIVES THE ROSE

Wang Jianlin gained immense wealth from his operations in commercial real estate and in the cultural field. This allowed him to become a generous philanthropist.

Wanda, under Wang Jianlin's guidance, has always emphasized its charitable contributions, as well as its achievements in the field of public interest. The company and the chairman's awards in the philanthropic sector are listed under 'corporate social responsibility' achievements on Wanda's official website.

When a 6.5 magnitude earthquake struck Ludian county in Zhaotong city, Yunnan province, on 3 August 2014, Wanda immediately decided to donate ¥10 million to the disaster-stricken area.

Wanda has already taken the lead many times in responding to natural disasters. After the massive earthquake in Wenchuan county, Sichuan province, in 2008, Wanda immediately donated ¥5 million. This sum was thereupon repeatedly increased, reaching a total sum of ¥359 million. When five south-western provinces, including Yunnan, Guangxi and Sichuan, were struck by the worst drought in a century, Wanda donated ¥40 million. Only a month later, in April 2014, Yushu county in Yushu Tibetan autonomous prefecture, Qinghai province, was struck by a 7.1 magnitude earthquake. Wanda donated ¥100 million to the quake-damaged area.

Since its foundation, Wanda has donated more than ¥3.7 billion to philanthropic causes over the course of more than 20 years. This is the largest amount of any private business in China. Wanda has been awarded the China Charity Award, given by the Ministry of Civil Affairs, seven times – more times than any other private business.

Wang Jianlin's contribution to philanthropy and the public good has won many honours. He is the honorary president of the China Charity Awards Association. He has also won the title of 'Model Individual for Supporting the Handicapped and Disabled', awarded by the State Council, as well as the title of 'Model Individual in Earthquake Relief Work' by the CCPCC, the State Council and the Central Military Commission.

Wang Jianlin has also taken an active part in bringing innovation to the philanthropic sector. In 2013, Wang Jianlin launched a charitable programme under the name 'student entrepreneurship contest'. The programme is planned to stretch over a period of ten years, up until 2023. A total of ¥500 million is pledged to be invested. Each year, a hundred outstanding start-up entrepreneurial teams or individuals are chosen. Each is rewarded with a start-up capital of ¥500,000, which adds up to a yearly investment of ¥50 million.

Furthermore, Wanda established a core value system which professes that "material value is subordinate to individual value, individual value is subordinate to corporate value, and corporate value is subordinate to social value." In other words, social value is the most important value for Wanda. If there is a conflict between the interests of an individual, corporation and society, then Wanda must do that which is in the interest of society. Wanda has always emphasized the need for shouldering social responsibility.

In the early days of the company, Wanda was in the initial phase of development and certainly had no excess of money. However, when Wang Jianlin heard that the teachers in the Xigang district in Dalian wanted to build a kindergarten but lacked adequate funds, he gritted his teeth and donated ¥1 million from the company's modest cash flow.

In 1991, Wanda provided ¥2 million to rebuild the People's Square, converting the cement-covered area into a green space. At the same time Wanda also bought the irrigation equipment needed for the upkeep of the square. In those days, domestically produced irrigation equipment only cost ¥700,000, but it had a very short service life.

When Wang Jianlin learned this, he resolutely decided to buy imported platinum irrigation equipment – it could last for over 30 years and it was computer-operated. Although the technology used was comparatively advanced, the price was also accordingly high – ¥2 million. Looking back, Wang Jianlin's decision was very wise: the imported irrigation equipment has now been in use for 22 years and it is still in good condition.

In 1993, Wanda donated ¥20 million for the construction of Dalian Xigang Stadium. In those days this was an astronomical figure, but Wang Jianlin was more concerned with building up Dalian.

As Wanda increasingly grew, its philanthropic activities also witnessed an enlargement. In August 2008, upon hearing news of the massive landslides in Zhouqu county in Gansu province, Wanda immediately called its the board of directors together to discuss the matter. In the end, Wanda decided to donate ¥10 million to the Zhouqu area via the China Charity Federation.

According to some sources, Wanda's donation of ¥10 million was the first significant sum of money the disaster-hit Zhouqu county received in the wake of the landslides. Wand's determination to be in the forefront reflects a deep love for the motherland as well as a steadfast upholding of morality.

Wanda also placed emphasis on philanthropy in education. Since its foundation, Wanda has donated funds for the building of over 40 "Hope" primary and middle schools. An example is the Wanda-funded Huafu Middle School. Originally, Wanda was planning to build a primary school. Research, however, showed that there was a surplus of primary schools in the Xigang district, but the area was short of middle schools. Wanda thereupon decided to increase its investment by ¥50 million and built a middle school instead of a primary school – Huafu Middle School, in a prime location in Dalian city centre.

Wanda also built a swimming pool, tennis courts and an indoor gym for Huafu Middle School. It was very uncommon in China for a middle school to have such lavish facilities.

In 2003, Wanda donated ¥50 million for the construction of a middle school affiliated to Changchun Normal University. Once built, the total area of the school reached 40,000 square metres, which included 48 classrooms.

Wanda has also donated money to universities. For example, in 1994 the group gave ¥500 million in donation to Dalian University. At that time Dalian University had only recently come into being as result of the merging of the Dalian Institute of Technology, Dalian Medical College and Dalian Teacher Training College. The facilities of the newly formed university were below standard and the university was issued with a yellow-card warning by the Ministry of Education. Furthermore, the Ministry of Education decided the university no longer had the right to enrol students. In view of this situation, Dalian city government hoped that Wanda, as one of the most advanced enterprises in the city, might be able to donate funds to the university to facilitate a prompt building of a new campus.

Wanda was under a lot of pressure at that time, but in the end it successfully managed to resolve all existing problems and construct a new campus for Dalian University. Wanda subsequently donated ¥25 million to Dalian University.

As well as all this, Wanda considers its employees' charitable activities to be on a par with the company's own achievements. In Wanda Group, employees' charitable work is closely linked to their performance. Charitable work, like contributions to the company, generates rewards and promotions. Wanda has drawn up a list of standards and regulations to govern the system of rewards.

One of Wanda's employees is Yang Ying, who works in the real estate department. When he first started working at Wanda, his monthly salary was just over ¥1,000. Although his salary was not very high, he still made the effort to spare some of his free time for charitable work. At the weekends, he used to go to 'Love at the Seaside' children's village to give free lessons to local children. As the village was located far from Dalian city centre, Yang Ying had to spend several hours on public transport, taking multiple buses. He moved house several times to make the journey more convenient, in order to be able to look after the children better. And so it was that Yang Ying quietly provided the children with compulsory education. After two years his colleagues brought up his story at a company presentation and only then did the company management find out about his charitable deed. As a result, his salary was doubled and he was promoted to deputy manager of the real estate department.

Naturally, Yang Ying's story is not the only example. Li Jianmin is the deputy general manager of Wanda Nanchang real estate. He has been doing charitable work for over ten years and has even sponsored the studies of dozens of orphans who had dropped out of school. He had, however, never told anyone about all this.

Li Jianmin once had business to do away from the office. As he passed over Ganjiang bridge, he saw a van rolling down the bank into the river. There were plenty of witnesses to the accident and many onlookers surrounded the scene, yet no one stretched out a helping hand. Upon taking in the scene, Li Jianmin immediately got out of his car and jumped down the embankment to save the driver. It was raining that day and the embankment was steep and slippery and over 10 metres high. It was no easy thing to pull the driver up. Li Jianmin did not give up, though. He gathered all his strength, he crouched down and pulled and pushed until he finally managed to drag the man up.

Coincidentally, a reporter from Nanchang TV happened to be passing by, and filmed Li Jianmin rescuing the man from the river. Later on, when the story was broadcast by Nanchang TV, Wanda management found out about Li Jianmin's brave deed. When they got to know him better, they discovered that he had been working for charities for ten consecutive years; they also learned of Li Jianlin's sponsorship of orphans. Wanda's leadership had deep admiration for Li Jianmin – it is not hard to do a good deed occasionally, but to persist in it for ten years is no easy feat.

In order to commend Li Jianmin, Wanda invited him to give a speech at Wanda Group's annual general meeting. The leadership then praised him and urged other employees to learn from him. In addition, Li Jianmin's salary was increased to the next level up and he was promoted to general manager.

Wanda's strong sense of social responsibility is reflected in its reward system for employees who do good deeds. Charity has become common practice with Wanda employees. Many companies find themselves in the situation where the boss participates in charitable activities that benefit society, but the company's employees take no active part in it. In truth, charitable work is not only the chairman's concern. It is important to create an atmosphere of commonplace charitable work within the company in order to nurture the loving hearts of every one of the company's employees.

Wanda's corporate culture is centred on benefiting society and shouldering social responsibility. Under the influence of such corporate culture, charitable work among Wanda employees is widespread. Each year, new Party members also embrace this spirit, as if to pass on the knowledge to younger generations, and have taken the initiative in donating funds to poor regions and sponsoring the education of orphans. In addition, each of Wanda's subsidiaries has set up a volunteering station. Each Wanda employee is required to do at least one hour of voluntary work a year.

The charitable trend that prevails among Wanda's employees was only made possible because of the way in which Wanda attaches importance to and supports charitable acts through establishing a strong, long-lasting corporate culture.

AFTERTHOUGHTS

Wanda's many different lines of business are the result of the company's horizontal diversification development strategy. They all face the same opportunities and pitfalls, be they Wanda department stores, Wanda cinemas, Wanda commercial real estate properties or Wanda Tourism holdings and luxury hotels. In reality, the greatest risk Wanda faces is difficult to overlook. It comes in the form of business cycles.

During the past 30 years, the rapid development of China's economy has been a crucial element in the rise of the

Wanda Group. Similarly, the recent economic downturn will pose a serious threat.

The downturn will affect Wanda's main lines of revenue, especially the sale of residential and commercial real estate. In addition, Wanda department stores, hotels and tourist sector will also suffer a major blow. The Wanda Group's industry characteristics and business volume make the company even more dependent on business cycles.

There are diverging views within society on the future of China's economic development in regard to the real estate market since 2012. Rapid changes of opinion have had far-reaching consequences.

Regarding Wuxi's Wanda Cultural Tourism City, Wang Jianlin has accused those who predicted the collapse of having ulterior motives. He, on the other hand, was very optimistic about the future of China's economy. He believed that because China's level of urbanization was only at 51%, this meant that a further 250 million people were yet to move to the cities before China reached a level of 75% – the same level as developed countries in the West. This presented a massive demand pool yet to be tapped.

Wang Jianlin's optimism even led him to predict that the size of the Chinese economy was going to overtake that of the US by the year 2022 to become the world's largest. It was on this basis that Wanda Group continued investing large sums of money in growth.

The figures for 2014, however, revealed an evident decline in the real estate market. In first-tier cities – Beijing, Shanghai, Guangzhou and Shenzhen – the volume of sales had declined by almost 30%. Consequently, large amounts of inventory and vast numbers of empty housing units led to widespread fiscal tightening measures within the real estate industry. A good number of developers went bankrupt as their cash flows ran dry.

Wang Jianlin's predictions only referred to theoretical growth potential. In fact, in the world history of economic development, it was rare to see a country that could retain continual growth for 30 years, as China had. Wang Jianlin's projection of continuing growth for another 20 years was almost unheard-of.

According to the figures published by the National Bureau of Statistics on 16 July 2014, the total floor space of commercial housing sold was 483.65 million square metres for the first half of 2014, which was a 6% decrease from the previous year. The revenue from sales equalled ¥3.1 trillion, which was a decrease of 6.7% compared to the same time the previous year. It is clear that the development of the real estate sector had slowed down and the speed of investment had decreased.

The real estate sector had witnessed a "great leap forward" in recent years. In addition, many real estate developers that sought to imitate the Wanda way, such as Joy City Property, R&F Properties and others, had entered the market. Consequently, not only did the sales slow, but it also became more difficult to attract investment. Rents were also pushed down as a result. All of this posed a direct threat to Wanda.

Since June 2014, more than ten local governments have cancelled purchasing restrictions on houses. The central government introduced a quantitative easing policy in which the central bank lowered the reserve ratio for China Development Bank. This injected more money into the economy and furthered the rebuilding of shanty towns, the expansion of high-speed rail and other infrastructure projects. It was expected that the monetary policy was gradually going to loosen. From Wanda's point of view, such policies reduced capital and financial costs in the short term. At the same time, they helped to prop up Wanda's various industries, such as the real estate sector.

While the commercial landscape was governed by business cycles, e-commerce transformed the commercial model. All these developments posed great external challenges to the Wanda commercial model. As for Wang Jianlin and his Wanda, they faced two further important challenges: how should the Wanda management structure maintain efficacy, and how should Wanda keep hold of its ever-expanding commercial empire?

During the early days, Wanda's management model was based on that of Wal-Mart. It was an operating model with a centralized form of management. With time, assets and operating scale multiplied day by day and the business increasingly expanded into more regions, yet at the same time it became more fragmented. In such a situation, if Wang Jianlin wished to hold his ground, he had no choice but to pay more attention to business management, organizational adjustments and risk control.

Currently, there is a total of ten core departments in Wanda's management structure: strategic management, investment management, financial management, HR management, leasing, planning, project management, marketing, operational management and information.

Wanda's information management system consists of infrastructure, an information portal and management platforms. It provides a platform for the bidding system, a project process management system, an operational management system, a sales management system, financial management and an HR management system. The office automation system serves as a work platform for coordinating all that goes on within Wanda Group. Its major functions include document management, process approval management and press release coordination.

Wanda Group employs over 100,000 people. It has business in more than 90 cities across China as well as having wholly-owned subsidiaries across the world. As the business spans the commercial real estate sector, department stores, cultural tourism, e-commerce, investment and finance, the management challenge this poses is immense. How can one maintain efficacy and encourage innovation within such a massive organization? How can the company be prevented from falling into the bureaucratic trap characteristic of large enterprises? The successful resolving of such questions can be attributed to Wang Jianlin.

Contrary to the popular opinion that Wang Jianlin has moved away from key decision-making, recent media reports have suggested that he is still at the heart of Wanda and that, as ever, Wanda's major policy decisions largely depend on him. Since Wanda is a not a public company, the outside world can only ever have an incomplete impression of what is going on within, so there is insufficient evidence to form any firm conclusions.

Wanda Group is still Wang Jianlin's private company. Even though Wanda's subsidiaries, Wanda Commercial Properties and Wanda Film Holdings, are equity carveouts, Wang Jianlin still remains the controlling shareholder. In terms of equity, Wanda Group is a 'family business'.

A management problem that the group still faces today is a shortage of available talent. As Wanda's industry scope increased in variety, lack of suitable talent remained a hotly debated issue within the company. When an enterprise reaches a certain point in growth, especially if it is an enterprise that operates in multiple industries, then talent gradually becomes the most important resource. Wang Jianlin stated that in order to find the right people, he was willing to search the whole world. Wanda would spare no financial reward in attracting the right talent.

There are 50 or so headhunting companies that channel talent in Wanda's direction. In addition, in order to resolve the problem of lack of talent, Wanda established the 'Wanda College', which helps to nurture interdisciplinary talent.

Though still full of vigour and ready to work for Wanda Group for many more years to come, Wang Jianlin already has a designated successor – his only son, Wang Sicong. Wang Sicong was educated in Great Britain. He is on the board of directors of Wanda Group but also runs his own investment company. It is said that Wang Jianlin gave him ¥500 million to start a business, on the basis that if he lost all of the starting capital, he would have no choice but to work for Wanda.

At the time of writing, however, Wang Sicong's investments have turned out well. In addition, using his aura as the son of the richest man in China, he has managed to gather a good number of fans on Weibo and similar social media platforms. He has developed a unique style of engaging in public debate. Although this kind of celebrity status might not be in accordance with Wang Jianlin's hopes, it makes him more than capable of becoming Wang Jianlin's painstakingly nurtured successor. When the need arises, he can step in to pick up the baton and take his place at Wanda's helm. For the time being there is no need to worry: Wang Jianlin is still in his prime and has no plans to leave.

APPENDICES

TRANSCRIPTS OF
TWO RECENT PUBLIC
SPEECHES
BY WANG JIANLIN

APPENDIX 1

REPORT ON THE WORK OF WANDA GROUP IN 2015

(XISHUANGBANNA, YUNNAN PROVINCE, 16 JANUARY 2016)

Today, we are holding Wanda Group's 2015 annual meeting at the resort that we have built in the beautiful city of Xishuangbanna. Yesterday, we all had a chance to visit the resort and try out what it has to offer. I believe everyone is still immersed in the joyful surprise. Here, I, on behalf of 130,000 Wanda employees, would like to extend a warm welcome to all representatives attending the annual conference.

There are two parts to my report today:

PART I: REVIEW OF MAJOR ACHIEVEMENTS IN 2015

In 2015, both the Chinese and global economies continued to worsen. The world was faced with severe new threats in the form of terrorism. Without doubt, we were facing many problems. Despite such dire circumstances, Wanda Group still performed well. This was thanks to the correct decisions made by the board of directors, the outstanding work carried out by the executive team headed by president Ding and, most importantly, thanks to the joint effort of all Wanda employees.

WANDA OUTPERFORMED ITS ANNUAL TARGETS

In 2015, the value of Wanda Group's total assets (according to cost method data) reached ¥634 billion, which is a 20.9% increase from last year. Total revenue equalled ¥290.16 billion, outperforming the annual plan by 9.3% and up by 19.1% from last year. The estimated net profit (unaudited) is also predicted to be significantly higher than last year.

Wanda Group's subsidiary Wanda Commercial Properties Company had an annual revenue of ¥190.45 billion, fulfilling the annual target by 101.3%. This was a 4.4% increase from last year. Of this, the revenue from real estate contracts was ¥164.08 billion, fulfilling 101.5% of the annual target with a 2.5% increase from last year. There were 26 newly opened Wanda Plazas. Wanda Plazas' total rental revenues reached ¥14.4 billion, 101.1% fulfilling the annual target with a 30.7% increase from last year. This is good news. Due to the substantial increases in rent, rent collection rate and property management fee collection rate were up 100%. Net rental profit as a percentage of net Wanda Commercial Properties profit is expected to exceed 35%, which is a 5% increase from 2014. Wanda Commercial Management Co. Ltd achieved a rental collection rate of 100% for three consecutive years. Ten new hotels were opened this year with a total number of 21,961 guest rooms. Annual revenue from hotels equalled ¥5.24 billion, achieving 101% of annual targets. This is 22.5% up from last year. Hotel owners' profit reached ¥710 million, meeting targets by 119.7% with a 22.4% increase from last year. 4.755 million square metres of property were added, bringing the total property area to 26.321 million square metres (excluding property owned by Wanda Group).

Wanda remains in the lead worldwide. There were 4.62 billion visits to Wanda Plazas and Ffan partner shopping malls. Of these, visits to Wanda Plazas added up to 2.03 billion. Wanda Commercial Properties successfully hosted the ninth Wanda Annual Commercial Conference. Over 3,000 businesses and more than 10,000 people attended the conference. The conference evolved from a mere company meeting to an industry-wide event that provided both an online as well as offline platform, fully accessible to the outside world. Wanda Commercial Properties is hosting the tenth annual conference this year. Ten is a significant milestone. I hope Commercial Management does a good job of hosting this year's annual conference. Revenues from Wanda Commercial Properties' other lines of business added up to ¥6.73 billion.

Wanda Cultural Industry Group's annual revenue reached ¥51.28 billion, completing 114% of the annual target and rising 45.7% compared to last year. AMC Theatres outperformed its annual targets. Wanda Cinemas' revenue added up to ¥8 billion, achieving 120.4% of the annual target and increasing 49.9% from last year. The box revenue totalled ¥6.3 billion, with a 49.6% increase from last year. Wan Club membership hit more than 50 million members, which was a 50% increase from last year. Each month, over 20,000 new members joined. Some 65% of box office revenue came from online sales, which shows that Wanda Cinemas has become an established online enterprise. Revenue from Wan Club members makes up over 80% of total revenue from box office sales, which means that stable income for Wanda Cinemas constitutes the majority of the total income. Another 942 new screens were added in the past year, bringing the total number of screens to 2,557. Wanda Cinemas' attendance rate was 1.9 times higher than the industry average. Revenue per screen was 2.1 times higher than the industry average.

Wanda Pictures had ¥6.15 billion in box office receipts, fulfilling targets to 180% with a 36.1% increase from last year. Despite being established only two years ago, Wanda Pictures ranked first nationwide in terms of the two key indicators – box office receipts and revenue. It invested in films like *A Hero or Not*, *Go Away Mr. Tumor* and *The*

Ghouls that have reaped the twin rewards of good word of mouth and box office receipts.

Box office receipts from films distributed by Wuzhou Film Distribution reached ¥6.7 billion, which accounted for 25% of the entire domestic market. Annual revenue was ¥1.65 billion, surpassing the annual target by 83.7%. Only a year after the establishment of Wuzhou Film Distribution, box office receipts and revenue ranked first in China among private companies.

Wanda Group wishes to extend praise to the outstanding work carried out by Wanda Cinemas, Wanda Pictures and Wuzhou Film Distribution as well as to Vice President Ye Ding, who oversees the three subsidiaries. The general managers of these three companies have already been promoted in the run-up to the annual conference. There is an old saying in Wanda that goes: "Working well at Wanda is the best connection you could have." There are five principles for talent management at Wanda. One of these is to simplify interpersonal relations. This is why anyone who does good work at Wanda will get promoted. I implore every unit in Wanda Group to learn from these three companies. For many years now, no individuals or companies were separately praised at Wanda's annual conference. The performance of these three companies, however, is indeed outstanding. For that reason, I am making an exception.

Wanda Tourism achieved an annual revenue of ¥12.02 billion, outperforming the annual target by 11.7% with a 59.8% increase on last year.

Wanda Sports Holdings reached an annual revenue of ¥5.87 billion, outperforming its annual target by 32.7%.

Wanda Kidsland opened 51 new fun parks, bringing the total number to 60. Wanda Kidsland's annual revenue reached ¥220 million, outperforming its target by 3.6%.

Other revenues from Wanda Cultural Industry amounted to ¥3.81 billion.

Wanda Financial Group revenue was ¥20.89 billion, outperforming the annual target by 597%. Considering that Wanda Financial Group was only just established, I will not go into details here regarding the performance of each of its subgroups.

The revenue of Wanda Department Stores reached ¥23.05 billion, outperforming the annual target by 2.3% with an 11.1% increase on last year. Wanda Group's other sources of revenue brought in ¥4.5 billion.

It is very encouraging to see that not a single one of the units within Wanda has fallen behind. All units have outperformed their annual targets. In view of the dire state of the Chinese economy, these results prove the prowess of Wanda's executive capacity. I hope that everybody present will continue to work hard in order to be able to rejoice each year at the annual conference.

THE INITIAL ACHIEVEMENTS OF ENTERPRISE TRANSFORMATION

The service industry revenue saw steep growth. In 2015, the Wanda service industry segment constituted 43% of total Wanda Group revenues, which is a 10% increase from last year. The revenue from the real estate sector remains almost constant without any significant growth.

Commercial rental revenues rose sharply, increasing by over 30%. Profits from commercial rental revenue are expected to constitute 35% of total profits. Judging by the speed of growth, Wanda commercial rental profit will constitute more than 50% of total profits.

Wanda Group paved the way for the 'asset-light' model. Firstly, Wanda initiated the partnership model for Wanda Plazas. In the past, Wanda bought all land and managed all investment. All property and rental income belonged to Wanda alone. After Wanda launched the asset-light strategy last year, a crowd of investors came calling on Wanda's door, willing to provide land and funds. Wanda provided brand and took charge of design, construction, tenant provision and operational management. Rental revenues were to be split according to a 7:3 ratio, with Wanda taking 30%. This ratio is rarely seen in the commercial field across the world. Usually, a brand operator can take at most 15–20% of the rental revenue. Wanda Commercial Properties has already signed three contracts in Beijing and Dalian that make use of the partnership model. Wanda Group executives, along with top executives from Wanda Commercial Properties, discovered that the Wanda brand is valuable. They decided to base the future direction of the asset-light development of Wanda Commercial Properties on the Wanda Plazas partnership model. There are two main advantages to this model: firstly, it is a zero-risk model. Land and funds are provided by other parties. Moreover, Wanda requires the right to designate the construction teams for the partnership project construction. All equipment used must be selected from the first-class brands in Wanda's brand base, so as to prevent the adverse effects of poor construction quality on future operational management. Secondly, Wanda does not need to worry about capitalization. It simply takes care of the construction and management of the project.

Moreover, the finished Wanda Plazas are sold to investors at cost price, so the price of construction is recovered.

Rental revenue is then split according to the 7:3 ratio between investors and Wanda. So far, we have signed asset-light partnership contracts on 20 out of the 25 Wanda Plazas that have opened this year. Why are the investors willing to agree to a split ratio of 7:3? It is because asset-light Wanda Plazas are a scarce resource on the Chinese market. They incur stable revenues with a low risk. Profit margins for rental income on asset-light Wanda Plazas go into double digits. On the surface, the investors can only gain around 7% rate of return. If, however, the investors were to buy land themselves, they might not even get the 7% return rate they get from Wanda. The reason Wanda can achieve such a high rate of return is, firstly, that the Wanda brand is extremely influential and enjoys nationwide popularity, so Wanda gets prime rates on land. The second reason is that Wanda constructs projects in bulk and implements centralized purchasing, which significantly decreases the costs. Lastly, Wanda has revamped the design of asset-light Wanda Plazas. Previously, around 55% of all floor space was available for use. Now it has risen to over 60%, increasing the rental area.

RAPID GROWTH OF THE CULTURAL INDUSTRY

Wanda has already become the industry leader. Wanda Cultural Industry Group was only set up three years ago. Ever since then, annual revenue has been rapidly increasing by ¥10 billion each year. In 2015, the company's revenue was equal to the sum of the revenues of the remaining top ten enterprises. Looking ahead, the revenue gap is set to increase even further. Wanda Cultural Industry Group has now become a deserving nationwide industry leader. This applies regardless, be it in terms of its brand influence, size of revenue or extent of internationalization.

Wanda Cultural Industry Group is diversified into four sectors, namely film, sport, tourism and children's entertainment. Of these four branches, three rank top in the world in terms of revenue, while the revenue from tourism ranks top within China. The sport sector has reached the top spot in the world with the help of mergers and acquisitions. There were no major enterprises in the children's entertainment sector in the first place, so Wanda naturally took the top rank. After Wanda Pictures acquired Legendary Pictures in 2016, it also became the worldwide film industry leader, ranked by revenue. We have already set a goal for the tourist segment: by 2020, the revenue from the tourist industry is to exceed 100 billion and the number of tourist visits is to rise to 200 million. Lastly, we want to become the largest tourism enterprise in the world. How can we achieve this goal? Wanda is now in the process of constructing large-scale tourist resorts around the country. Three of these large-scale tourist resorts have already been opened. Apart from the one in Wuhan, the remaining two are in relatively remote regions where transport is still a problem. Starting this year, however, we are going to open large-scale tourist resorts in easily accessible, developed cities. The number of tourists should see a sharp rise. With so many large-scale tourist resorts, by 2020 Wanda must be sure to rank top in the world.

The diversification into these four industries does not mean that Wanda Group will not enter additional fields in the future. If we come across suitable resources, it is not out of the question for us to enter a new field through mergers and acquisitions.

JOINT ONLINE AND OFFLINE DEVELOPMENT

It is very encouraging to see that in 2015, Wanda Group launched the 'internet+' development model, which combines online and offline development. In the film and TV industry, Wanda is involved in film production, distribution and film screening, including the movie website Mtime. Within the tourist industry, Wanda boasts large-scale tourist resorts as well as China's largest offline travel agency. Wanda also invests in Tongcheng Tourism Group. At the company's bidding, the children's entertainment sector has also started exploring an integrated model of physical stores combined with animation production and online stores. The art of growing the children's entertainment sector is not in opening several hundred retail stores or in simply selling members' cards. We must incorporate retail stores with animation production, and we must also provide online services, including the introduction of intellectual property (IP) product sales and so on.

Wanda has obtained a good number of IP rights. In 2015 Wanda applied to both Chinese and international governments and relevant departments for 470 patents and IP rights. In total, Wanda gained 1,330 patents and IP rights in 2015. Although we applied for only 470, we obtained permission for 1,330. This is because in the past we applied for many more. Up until now Wanda has accumulated 4,219 patents and IP rights worldwide. The majority of these are in the cultural field. These will serve as the fundamental guarantee for the rapid take-off of the Wanda cultural industry sector.

Wanda gained two major achievements. The first is that Wanda Cinemas was successfully launched and became the first stock among Chinese cinema chains. From going public on January 1 to the end of the year, the stock price multiplied 10.2 times, which made it the most valuable cinema chain on the world cinema chain stock market. It was selected to be used for the China Securities Index (CSI) 300 index. I saw an American post on Facebook, saying: "The world's best company is Wanda Cinemas. It is a shame that Americans can't afford to buy it." However, Wanda Cinemas should not be overly proud. Apart from your own efforts, the fundamental reason for your success is that you were able to catch the golden era of development for the Chinese film industry.

The second of our major achievements is the opening of the Xishuangbanna Resort. The Xishuangbanna Resort is a masterpiece of the Wanda cultural tourism sector. It is fundamentally different from the cultural tourism projects in Wuhan and Changbaishan. The theme park and Wanda Plaza at the Xishuangbanna Resort are strongly influenced by local culture. To expand our business in China, we must make each project reflect local characteristics. I daresay that the three five-star hotels in the Xishuangbanna Resort are masterpieces within the mountain resort hotel sector worldwide. The Dai nationality show and the theme park are of first-class world standard. The Kunming high-speed railway which connects China, Laos and Thailand is set to open in 2018. One of the high-speed railway stops will be located only two or three kilometres away from the Xishuangbanna Resort. As the new line will connect to China's high-speed rail network, it will only take five hours from Chengdu, just over three hours from Chongqing, and only two hours from Kunming. Tourists from Guangdong and Shenzhen will also be able to visit conveniently. I trust that in time, the Xishuangbanna

Resort will prove to be very popular, so much so that tourists will compete over booking rooms.

WANDA FINANCIAL GROUP ESTABLISHED

The Wanda Financial Group was established in Shanghai with a registered capital of ¥10 billion. The group is diversified into internet finance, the Feifan retail platform, insurance and investment. In the foreseeable future Wanda Financial Group is set to diversify further.

We have explored internet finance options. Wanda's online-to-offline (O2O) platform has been going through an exploratory phase. At times, it was a bumpy ride. Currently, the internal management have agreed to focus first on the launching of internet finance. O2O platforms of other companies are making losses. They can only be kept afloat with the help of constant investment from the shareholders. As I said before, it is unthinkable for a company in any industry to rely on shareholders' investment to remain functional. Wanda's ventures in internet finance must bring in revenue and profit. It must be able to fend for itself. We shall first focus on expanding the Ffan card [see next paragraph], which is a key link in bringing together all internet finance lines of business. Once the Ffan card is in wide use, we shall turn our attention to other fields. We must not attempt to try to develop everything at once. Ffan launched the external partnership model in October last year. Within less than three months of operation, 70 contracts with large shopping centres were signed as part of the external partnership model. An additional 130 or more Wanda Plazas have brought the total number of Ffan internet shopping centres to more than 600. In 2015, 4.62 billion visits were recorded. Over 100 million consumers were reached through the Ffan O2O platform.

We have established partnerships with large financial institutions. Last year we reached partnership agreements with major financial institutions. We added the credit card function to our Ffan card. The Ffan card offers a broad range of functions such as online parking space reservation, seat reservation and queuing reservation as well as special offers, point collection system, cash deposit function, currency exchange and credit card function. With so many functions contained within a single card, Ffan is the world's first multifunction financial service card.

CONSIDERABLE ACHIEVEMENTS IN MERGERS & ACQUISITIONS

We acquired high-quality assets. In 2015, Wanda made transnational acquisitions of Infront Sports & Media, World Triathlon Corporation, Hoyts Group and Legendary Pictures. Wanda also invested in the Spanish football club Atlético Madrid. In total, Wanda's annual overseas investment added up to more than US$5 billion. Up until 30 December 2012, Wanda's total overseas investment reached US$15 billion, of which US$10 billion was in the US. In 2012, Wanda acquired AMC Theatres. When I was in America, I said that "In the next ten years, Wanda will invest a minimum of US$10 billion in the United States." When reporting the story, a well-known American media company added a caption: "We hope that Mr Wang will fulfil his promise," meaning to say, "Do not fool with the American people." Three years have passed since then and our investment in the US has already exceeded

US$10 billion. I plan to have another article published in the American press: "Wanda fulfilled its investment commitment – ahead of time." On the domestic market, Wanda acquired companies such as Aeon Life Insurance and Shimao Cinema Line.

It also invested in LY.com and Mtime. Wanda's investment on the domestic market surpassed ¥10 billion. Wanda's mergers and acquisitions, both domestic and overseas, are high-quality assets. Some of these even count among scarce resources. For example, Infront Sports & Media serves as an agent with exclusive broadcasting rights for the FIFA World Cup in Asia. Infront is the exclusive partner of seven major winter sports international federations, including skiing, ice-skating and ice-hockey federations. It holds the right to market and broadcast their events. The World Triathlon Corporation is the sole owner of the Ironman brand. It has a more than 90% share in the long-distance triathlon market worldwide.

As the number of mergers & acquisitions started increasing, the influence of the Wanda International brand has become more and more evident. For example, I have attended one-on-one meetings with important political figures worldwide, including the president of the US and the British Prime Minister. I have also met with the CEO of Goldman Sachs and other top-class entrepreneurs around the world. I had the honour of being elected as the vice-chairman of Harvard University's Global Advisory Council. Wanda's acquisition of Legendary Pictures had an especially far-reaching influence worldwide. Such response far exceeded our expectations. A spokesperson for the Chinese Ministry of Foreign Affairs stated that the Ministry would like to take advantage of Wanda's acquisition of Legendary Pictures to further expand Sino-American cultural exchange.

SYNERGIES ARISING FROM MERGERS AND ACQUISITIONS

Infront Sports & Media have paved the way for Wanda to enter the sport industry. This acquisition helped to show Wanda how things are done there. We do things differently to the way it is done on the domestic market. In China, some companies simply set up clubs and drown them with money. Wanda's strategy is to establish connections for upward expansion by acquiring international sport brands. Wanda's investments in LY.com and Mtime formed successful synergies with Wanda's existing businesses. In the film industry, Wanda is the only enterprise in the world to span the entire film network from production to distribution and screening. Within the tourism industry, Wanda is the only enterprise in China with large-scale tourist resorts that utilizes both online and offline forms of interaction with customers. However, in order to achieve the full potential of using the internet+ model, we rely on the hard work of our colleagues in the film and television sector as well as on those in the tourist sector. The internet+ model is not equivalent to simply using the internet; they are two completely different concepts.

Our M&A businesses have been performing well. In the run-up to the annual conference, Wanda confirmed that three cities in China are to host the international triathlon event – the Ironman. Due to the capacity limits of the International Triathlon Corporation, we cannot host in too many cities. We chose three cities and we signed the agreement for hosting large-scale international triathlons in these three cities this year. Infront Sports & Media will soon add two major events to the sports calendar in China. Legendary Pictures have agreed to assured five-year operational goals with Wanda Cultural Group. Hoyts Cinema Line is set to earn a profit this year. Aeon Life Insurance Company, which Wanda invested in, had been making a loss for the past eight years. Wanda is lucky, though: a year after our investment we are already seeing the company make a profit.

The reason the acquired businesses are in a healthy state is that Wanda is a giant business ecosystem with a powerful executive force. If a business has bright prospects, Wanda is willing to invest in a business that might momentarily be making a loss. We do not, however, stand for a business that is making a loss in the long term. It must be profitable, as profit is the fundamental guarantee of the market value of a company, thereby ensuring its survival. If there is no profit to show off, then no matter how good a story you try to sell, it won't work in the long term.

CONTINUAL IMPROVEMENTS IN ENTERPRISE MANAGEMENT

Management standards have risen. In 2015, president Ding along with eight of Wanda Group's departments launched the building information modelling (BIM) platform to aid with project management within the real estate business sector. BIM technology is specifically designed for the industrial sector. Wanda is the first enterprise in the world to successfully use the BIM technology in construction management projects and to implement a comprehensive system of smart management. This is revolutionary in the real estate industry around the world. Last year's pilot programme reduced the number of managers in Wanda by 10%, saving over ¥1 billion. The new technology helped to save on human resources, while at the same time increasing efficiency. More importantly, it helped to fix loopholes in the management system.

Wanda Commercial Properties have reformed the investor solicitation and management system. We have brought into effect a separation of powers between the three departments in charge of brand management, investor attraction and operations. This greatly decreased the powers of discretion existent within the system. Wanda's Huiyun information management system was upgraded to version 2.0. The upgrade and optimization of the system took place while ensuring complete operational security and utmost convenience. This system is very powerful: it enables the user to manage Wanda Plazas from anywhere around the world and at any time. All this is possible to do using a mobile-phone app. On a tour of the US, a member of the audience asked a Wanda Commercial Properties employee how the Wanda Plazas are managed, considering there are so many of them spread over an area larger than Europe. The Wanda manager took out his mobile phone where he was immediately able to see information on the revenue, foot traffic and security of any Wanda Plaza, regardless of its location. The audience was stunned. They had not thought that commercial management in China was so advanced.

Wanda incorporated a model of internal competition within its film and TV production unit. The film and TV production company introduced a system of interdepartmental competition in the production of internal projects. The aim is to ensure the quality of production by abiding by the laws of natural selection. As a result, the decision whether to launch a project does not lie solely with the film production unit. It is a joint decision between the three departments of film production, distribution and cinema chain that is arrived at by casting votes. Such a mechanism greatly reduced the risk involved in undertaking each project. This is why all films selected through this method in 2015 earned profits. In fact, this model is used in film production in Hollywood. When Wanda initially started using this model, there were many within the film industry who mocked us, saying they were the film professionals. If they said it would be a successful film, then it would; if not, then it wouldn't. Others laughed: "Wanda does not sign contracts with actors, nor do they engage talent recruitment agencies. Instead, they vote on filmmaking. Can that be called a film production company?" We have, however, already proved the superiority of our commercial model with facts. Wanda Film Holdings company is already ahead of industry competition. We plan to widen that gap further.

Wanda's Cultural Tourism Planning & Research Institute was identified as a high-tech enterprise by the Ministry of Science and Technology, the Ministry of Finance and the State Administration of Taxation. There are tens of thousands of planning and design firms in China, but Wanda is the first and only one to be designated a high-tech enterprise for its independent, innovative work. Although Wanda brought in foreign directors to take charge of the Han and Dai nationality shows, the buildings and equipment were mostly designed by Wanda. Starting with the Nanchang Wanda City, Wanda Cultural Tourism & Research Institute have developed the major facilities for the theme park, as well as other apparatus used in the cultural tourism sector. The institute owns a number of patents around the world.

Wanda has seen a change in the talent structure. Two thirds of Wanda's current senior executives are specialists outside of the real estate sector. There are ten non-Chinese senior executives who make up almost one quarter of senior management. A few years back, we started accompanying Wanda's interim, annual and any other major conferences with simultaneous interpretation. That is one of the subtle manifestations of Wanda's internationalization.

SETTING AN EXAMPLE FOR CORPORATE SOCIAL RESPONSIBILITY

Employment

In 2015, Wanda increased the number of jobs in the service sector by 105,000. Of these newly created jobs, 40,000 were graduate positions. This amounts to about 1% of the total number of posts created nationwide this year.

Entrepreneurship

Wanda supported 57 entrepreneurial graduate ventures. The success rate reached 95%. The reason we were able to achieve such a high rate of success is that Wanda has a specialist department with excellent service offering guidance for budding entrepreneurs.

Taxes

In 2015, Wanda Group paid ¥30.2 billion in taxes, which is a 10% increase from last year. There are only a handful of enterprises in China that pay over ¥30 billion each year.

Charity

In 2015, Wanda donated ¥360 million to charitable causes.

Poverty relief

Last year Wanda entered into a contract with Danzhai county in Guizhou province, becoming the first enterprise to commit to a poverty alleviation model whereby "an enterprise joins hands with a county in order to eradicate poverty". Last year we agreed to invest ¥300 million in building a vocational school with a capacity of 2,000 students. We have already obtained the necessary land and the building works are to start in March this year. This will be the first county-level vocational school nationwide.

Wanda achieved great results in 2015. There were, however, also a number of problems. To give you some examples, we occasionally grappled with employee corruption and a number of institutions were overstaffed. On some occasions, we struggled to avoid the pitfalls of being a large corporation. The phenomenon of reporting positive news but refraining from passing on negative news is still existent. I hope that senior executives at all levels will pay more attention to these problems and gradually find ways to resolve them. As our time is limited, I will not go deeper into these problems at the annual conference. We shall hold separate meetings to discuss and improve these deficiencies.

PART II: MAJOR WORK TARGETS FOR 2016

In 2016, Wanda Group aims to increase the value of its assets to ¥750 billion, with revenues adding up to ¥254.3 billion, which is a 12% decrease compared to 2015. The main reason for the decrease in revenue is that Wanda Commercial Properties has purposefully been decreasing real estate revenue since 2014. In 2014, real estate revenue dropped by ¥64 million. Assuming real estate revenue keeps decreasing by 10% each year, Wanda will see a real estate revenue drop of over ¥80 billion in 2016. On the other hand, Wanda Group's service industry revenue targets are to see a sharp rise.

Wanda Commercial Properties is expected to earn around ¥130 billion of revenue in 2016. Although the target revenue is forecast to drop, the net profit will retain double-digit growth. Revenue from real estate contracts is projected to be around ¥100 billion, while revenue from agreed partnerships is expected to reach ¥110 billion. Another 55 new Wanda Plazas will be opened. Compared to 2015, the number of new Wanda Plazas will double, with 55 scheduled to open this year. Rental revenue is expected to reach around ¥19.5 billion. Fourteen new hotels will go into operation, with a projected revenue of ¥6.14 billion. Property space is to increase by a further 580,000 square metres. Wanda plans to embark on 71 new projects. One of these projects will be in cultural tourism. Three asset-heavy Wanda Plazas are scheduled to open as well as 55 asset-light ones. I read in some articles that China's richest man is thinking of retiring from the real estate sector. The truth is, Wanda is not retiring from real estate. It is only that Wanda no longer considers the real estate industry to be the central pillar of its business. The real estate sector is no longer the major source of Wanda's revenue and profits. This is because of the cyclical nature of the real estate industry, which rises and falls over time. The global real estate trend suggests that the industry will start shrinking once the level of urbanization reaches 75% and home ownership climbs to 80%. Since Wanda needs a long-term, stable cash flow, we have no choice but to transition to other industries. Wanda Commercial Properties will continue to operate, but the volume of revenue will stabilize at around ¥100 billion without seeking further growth. Wanda will instead generate growth from other industries.

Wanda Cultural Group has an annual revenue target of ¥66.64 billion in 2016, which is a 30% increase. If we can reach this target, Wanda Cultural Group will count among the top ten enterprises in the global cultural industry, which would be very exciting. The revenue of AMC Theatres and Wanda Cinemas is projected to increase steadily. Wanda Cinemas is expected to reach a double-digit billion revenue in 2016. The reason why I am not being more specific with figures is that Wanda Cinemas have asked me to keep the actual figure a secret. A further 77 cinema cities are scheduled to open, bringing an additional 698 screens (excluding mergers and acquisitions). Wanda Pictures aims to bring in ¥1 billion of revenue this year, which is a 71% increase from 2015. Wuzhou Film Distribution is projected to earn ¥9 billion from box office receipts with revenue of ¥1.76 billion. This is a 10.6% increase from last year. I feel that such a target is too low; perhaps Wuzhou Film Distribution wants to play it safe, so that they can report they have outperformed their annual target next year. Wanda Tourism is expected to generate ¥16.1 billion in revenue. Wanda Theme Parks plans to bring in ¥1.77 billion of income while Wanda Children's Entertainment is aiming for ¥780 million. Wanda Sports Holdings is projected to generate ¥7 billion of revenue. Other income of Wanda Cultural Group is expected to add up to ¥730 million.

In 2016, Wanda Financial Group aims to generate income of ¥21.18 billion, of which ¥4.46 billion will be from internet finance. The number of active members in the internet finance database is projected to surpass 100 million, with 50 million new Ffan cards being issued. We hope to grow the number of large Ffan partner shopping centres by 1,000. This target was proposed directly by Ffan and it is no easy task.

Projected revenue of Aeon Life Insurance is ¥16.52 billion. [Our third-party payment platform] 99bill aims for target revenue of ¥4.01 billion. Wanda Investment Company will complete three major overseas and two domestic M&A operations (excluding cinema chains).

Wanda Department Stores will generate projected revenue of ¥17.53 billion in 2016. The business will achieve overall profitability, which will strengthen its future initial public offerings (IPOs). Revenue from other subsidiaries is expected to reach ¥4.92 billion.

IMPLEMENTING INITIAL STAGES OF ENTERPRISE TRANSFORMATION

In the course of the last century, there has not been a single large real estate enterprise that succeeded in undergoing comprehensive self-transformation. Wanda is on course to rewrite global economic history. We will be the first large real estate enterprise to successfully transform itself into a service-based enterprise. When we speak of transformation, we mean it. And 2016 is the key year for Wanda's transformation. We have set ourselves some main objectives:

The revenue and profit from the service sector must constitute over 50% of total revenues and profits. We aim that by the end of 2016, the two key indicators in the service sector, revenue and profit, will constitute at least 55%, maybe even 60%. By the end of the year, Wanda Group will no longer be known as a real estate enterprise. We will have become a cross-industry enterprise. It is estimated that by 2017, two thirds of Wanda Group's revenues and profits will come from the service industry. We will have completed our objectives for transformation a year ahead of what was originally planned.

FUNDAMENTAL CHANGES IN THE STRUCTURE OF WANDA COMMERCIAL PROPERTIES

By the end of 2016, Wanda Commercial Properties will strive to generate over 50% of total income from sources other than real estate. There will be substantial growth in revenue from overseas holdings. By the end of 2016, we aim for revenue from our overseas holdings to constitute 20% of total Wanda Group revenue.

EMPHASIS ON THE CULTURAL INDUSTRY

Adjusting development goals

When Wanda Cultural Group was established in 2012, we set targets for it to generate ¥40 billion in 2016 and 80 billion in 2020. In the end, revenue for 2015 already surpassed ¥50 billion, so our original targets seem far too low.

After some thought, we have adjusted the target for 2020 to ¥150 billion, with net profit reaching ¥12 billion. We have five years to achieve the target, yet the deciding moment will come within these coming two years. In five years time, Wanda Cultural Group will undoubtedly become a global industry leader. We aim to be ranked among the top five global cultural enterprises.

Promoting innovation and intellectual property

Wanda Culture Group's rapid growth is mainly due to an emphasis on innovation and intellectual property. Led by Wanda Cultural Tourism Planning & Research Institute, Commercial Planning Institute, Hotel Design Institute and other subsidiaries of Wanda Cultural Group, we must place innovation at the forefront. In particular, the two theme parks and four performances to be launched in the newly opened Wanda Cities in Nanchang and Hefei are expected to be a big sensation. Yesterday evening you all had a chance to watch the Dai nationality show. It was splendid. The performances in Nanchang and Hefei must be so stunning that when the curtain goes up, the audience is already clapping and cheering. That is what I call "high-level".

Hosting major sports events

In 2016, Wanda Sports Holdings should stage events in China in at least three different major sports. I emphasize three different sports, not just three events. We aim for two things: uniqueness and world-class standard. Either the event is the only one of its kind in China, or else there are sport events of that kind in China, but the difference is that ours are world-class events. Our level has to be higher than that of the existing domestic sport fixtures. We have already agreed for the Ironman triathlon to be held in three Chinese cities, but we have yet to confirm the remaining two. As we are currently going through a process of negotiations, we cannot yet announce the remaining two. Wanda either holds the intellectual property rights for these two events, or it shares the intellectual property rights with international sport organizations. What we are doing here is bringing world-class-standard sport events back to China.

Expanding the tourism business

Out of all enterprises in the world, Wanda is the only one to operate a full travel industry value chain. As part of its internet+ model, Wanda owns many large tourist resorts, offline travel agencies and online internet platforms. The only thing we are missing is an airline. In 2016, Wanda Theme Parks and Wanda Tourism Holdings need to focus on boosting profitability. This in particular means turning the three tourist resorts in Xishuangbanna, Nanchang and Hefei into huge sensations. The Nanchang and Hefei resorts enjoy favourable conditions. They are both connected to the high-speed rail network, as well as being regional transport hubs. In addition, they are located in China's central regions, which makes them easy to get to from anywhere around the country. However, in Xishuangbanna, accessibility still remains a problem. As a result, we should not rely on traditional approaches and should instead seek innovative solutions. Wanda also plans to complete two M&A operations in the tourist industry.

Ensuring the smooth opening of Wanda Cities in Nanchang and Hefei

In May, Nanchang Wanda City is scheduled to open and in September we will be opening the Wanda City in Hefei. This does not leave us a lot of time. We not only need to make sure that construction works are finished on time, we also need to observe that high quality standards are adhered to. The staff bonuses in the Cultural Project Centre are closely linked to the quality of construction as well as the rate of progress of each project. Before the cities are opened, we need to be absolutely sure that everything is safe. All equipment needs to adhere to US, EU and Chinese safety regulations. US and EU procedures are the strictest, which is why Wanda must be sure to pass them. This will be a guarantee of quality. We must also make all necessary preparations prior to the official opening to ensure a successful launch.

Promoting cultural brands overseas

This year, Wanda Cultural Tourism Cities are to be built in one or two developed countries. The asset-light model will be used. We are currently in the process of finalizing negotiations. This will be the first time that China exports a major cultural product to developed nations. It is a significant breakthrough for the Chinese tourist industry. Apart from American Disney, no other country has managed to produce a cultural product that would storm the global market. It took Disney half a century and yet there are fewer than 20 Disney resorts around the world. The Wanda City brand must do better than Disney. We will conquer the world. We will, however, certainly not replicate the Chinese version of the Wanda City in every country we venture into. Wanda Cities around the world must reflect the local characteristics of each destination. Why do I insist on this? It is because I want to change the way Chinese officials in some places have a blind faith in all things foreign. When Disney finally announced the opening of the Shanghai Disneyland, the whole project had taken over 20 years. I cannot even imagine how much the costs have gone up in that time. Our aim is to construct Wanda Cities in Wuxi and Guangzhou that will be superior to Disney's Disneyland. Measured by two key indicators – number of visitors and revenue – we aim for the Wanda City in Wuxi to surpass the Disneyland in Shanghai and for the Wanda City in Guangzhou to exceed the Disneyland in Hong Kong. China Central Television (CCTV) broadcasts a programme called *Topics in Focus*. The motto of the programme is 'Speaking with Facts'. Wanda, too, would like to 'speak with facts' to prove that, although in the past the Chinese people perhaps could not compete with foreigners, now the times have changed. Chinese people now, and especially in the future, are no worse than foreigners. Perhaps we can even do better than foreigners. This is what I call the Wanda spirit.

INNOVATION IN INTERNET FINANCE

Playing to our strengths

In our ventures into online to offline (O2O) commerce, we cannot replicate the models adopted by others. We must take advantage of Wanda's plentiful offline resources to create a model of our own. One of Wanda's advantages is that we have masses of offline commercial tenants and customers. In 2015, foot traffic reached 4.6 billion visits. This year, it is projected to surpass 10 billion. The greatest challenge online enterprises are facing is the fact that they have to spend money on diverting customer flow, which tends to be unstable. A slight faltering of service, and customers are gone. Wanda's customers are all regulars. They return every day. In addition, we have our e-commerce platform, Ffan, with its cloud-billing system that allows us to monitor our retailers' income flows. Thirdly, Wanda has countrywide on-site executive teams who are backed up by our extensive business management system. We have the resources we need. What remains to be seen is whether we can turn these into a business advantage and earn profits. The Financial Group should focus on working out the best way to connect our offline and online platforms.

Building a first-class credit reporting company

Wanda is ideally positioned to run a consumer credit reporting business, thanks to our access to a wealth of retailer and customer data. Wanda's consumer-related data is even more comprehensive than the data collected by e-commerce operators. The data reveals that each of Wanda's customers on average visits more than 50 times per year, which is about once a week. The purpose of customer visits is not limited to shopping, as visits for the purpose of eating, drinking and entertainment are also included. E-commerce customers mainly visit for the purpose of buying, which tends to be more of a one-off activity.

Developing internet financing

By 2020, Wanda's O2O commerce will have established partnerships with 5,000 large shopping centres. We will have access to 2 million retailers and will serve 700-800 million consumers in the cities. Even if only a small portion of consumers and retailers use our internet finance, it is still a sizeable number. Currently, the demand for internet financing is huge. The key problems are finding a source for loan money and reducing the costs involved. The majority of retailers on our e-commerce platform Ffan are small to mid-sized enterprises willing to take out low-cost loans, which resolves both of these problems. There is nothing now to hold us back.

Introducing a new all-purpose card

The Feifan All-Purpose Card offers a variety of functions integrated in one card whereby a customer can redeem special offers and collect points, deposit cash or exchange currency. It also doubles as a credit card. Now, with the support of major financial institutions, we shall strive to issue 50 million cards in 2016. The more cards we issue, the greater the source of capital for internet financing. We should learn from the experience of Yu'ebao and offer a slightly higher interest rate than them to attract capital. Many Chinese online payment platforms similar to Yu'ebao struggle to find appropriate investment channels for their capital, so they deposit their money in banks. Wanda, on the other hand, has millions of retailers and hundreds of millions of customers who are in need of loans. The key to solving many of our problems is to scale up the number of cards being issued.

CONTINUING WORK ON MERGERS AND ACQUISITIONS

Continue buying

People say that Wanda just keeps buying and buying, and that is exactly what we want to continue doing. In 2016, we are aiming to complete three major acquisitions overseas and two domestically (excluding cinema chains). Wanda Cinemas must take advantage of their prime position on the capital market to increase their domestic acquisitions of cinema chains.

Buying the right assets

We need to focus on enterprises that are relevant to Wanda's lines of business and that have the potential to strengthen our competitiveness. We should not be guided by the principle of buying whatever is cheap. We must buy that which is right for us. For example, Wanda's acquisition of Infront Sports and Media opened the door to the sport industry and helped us to find the right model of development for the industry. Soon after, we became a leading global sports enterprise. Let me remind you, though: we should strive to avoid using the Wanda brand when making acquisitions, as it appears that the Wanda brand of itself drives prices up.

Buying landmark properties

Wanda can invest in one to three landmark properties in cities around the world, but I emphasize the necessity of taking into consideration returns on our investments. Investments should only be made if we are sure of a positive return. Property managers of our overseas holdings should be selected on a competitive basis by inviting bids from management companies.

CONSTANTLY STRIVE TO IMPROVE ENTERPRISE MANAGEMENT

The competitiveness of an enterprise comes down to the nature of the company's management. Advanced technologies and lucrative business models could not be successfully implemented without meticulous management. Without sound management, a company would lose its competitiveness and would surely perish before long. Nowadays many Chinese companies exhaust their efforts in developing so-called internet-plus technologies and innovative business models. In my opinion, most of this is just talk. I am not saying we don't need revolutionary technologies or innovative business models. What I mean is that in the end it all comes down to whether or not a company has management capabilities and whether or not it can generate profit. Enterprise competitiveness is not something that can be determined overnight. Rather than thinking only of the present moment, we should look further afield. Can a company survive in 10 or 20 years from now? A company that has a long-term vision of stable cash flow is what I call an outstanding company.

Focusing on net profit

From now on, Wanda will not judge performance based on revenue. Instead, we shall monitor performance based on net profit and market value. Those who generate more profit, and those who create greater value for the company, will be the ones to be promoted. The four executives from the film industry that earned praise and promotion at this year's annual conference are an example of this.

Keeping costs in check

Last year, president Ding led efforts to adjust staffing levels. This year, we need to carry on implementing the changes. As Wanda gradually moves away from real estate to the service industry, keeping costs in check is a way of generating profits and strengthening our core competitive ability. In real estate, investment of several billion gets lost in the bigger picture. This is not so in the service industry. We need to make sure that we keep strict control of our costs and expenses. We have drawn a red line: the rate of increase of a company's costs must not be greater than the rate of increase of a company's profits. Each company can apply for permission for higher costs and expenses as long as the rise in profit outweighs the rise in costs.

Implementing BIM systems

BIM systems began to be implemented on a trial basis in January this year. Detailed rules and regulations will be finalized in the fourth quarter of 2016 to pave the way for official implementation of BIM systems in January 2017. Once in effect, Wanda will no longer have to invite bidders. Project costs can be estimated according to the location and product requirements of each project, which increases the accuracy of project management. In addition to benefits such as reducing staffing requirements, increasing efficiency and facilitating project management, BIM can also reduce the likelihood of corruption.

Upgrading the Huiyun Intelligent Management System to version 3.0

In 2016, we will have finalized the newest version of the Huiyun system. It will be launched in 2017, together with BIM systems. We aim for the Huiyun system to become the world's largest cloud-based intelligent management system.

Strengthening internal audit and supervision

Firstly, emphasis must be placed on prevention. We should focus on patching up existing loopholes. Secondly, we must increase the strictness of our supervision system. If necessary, wrongdoers must be punished, dismissed or sued. Thirdly, we shall make publicly available a list of employees who have been dismissed or who have been convicted of criminal offences. Corruption will not be tolerated.

CONTINUING TO TAKE THE LEAD IN CORPORATE SOCIAL RESPONSIBILITY

Employment: In 2016, we aim to create 100,000 new jobs, of which 40,000 will be graduate jobs.

Entrepreneurship: We hope to give support to 100 graduate entrepreneurs.

Tax: ¥30 billion will be paid in taxes in 2016.

Environment: We will start implementing the Wanda Green Building Energy Saving Plan 2016-2020. Wanda completed the 2011-2015 Green Building Plan, achieving all targets. Wanda secured one third of the total number of green building design and operation certificates granted in China between 2011 and 2015. This is far more than any other company. In future, all projects developed by Wanda must meet green building standards and secure design and operation certification.

Charity: In 2016, ¥400 million will be donated to charitable causes.

Poverty relief: Building works on the Danzhai County Vocational College of Technology are to start in March this year in order to ensure that the college can start enrolling students from midway through 2017. Wanda's poverty relief fund has gone into operation and will start distributing cash this year. Why do we have need of a poverty relief fund? The aim of the fund is to support the orphaned and the disabled who are unfit for work and cannot earn a living on their own. With regard to Wanda's industrial poverty relief projects, I will be visiting Dazhai county during the first quarter to attend face-to-face meetings with local representatives, finalizing the details. We will then aim for work to start on these projects within a year.

The board of directors is sincerely grateful for the hard work of all Wanda employees. Although at times working at Wanda may seem tiring, hard work will always be rewarded. This year, we achieved great results and exceeded our growth targets. With each passing year, Wanda is undergoing rapid changes.

I would also like to use this opportunity to thank the staff at Xishuangbanna holiday resort for the hard work they have done to make the annual conference possible. This is especially directed to the staff of Wanda Vista, Crown Plaza and DoubleTree by Hilton hotels.

The Chinese New Year of the Monkey is around the corner. Let me use this opportunity to wish everyone present, as well as all our colleagues at Wanda, a happy and prosperous new year!

Thank you!

APPENDIX 2

GOING GLOBAL
– THE WANDA WAY

(SAÏD BUSINESS SCHOOL, OXFORD
UNIVERSITY, 23 FEBRUARY 2016)

It is a great honour to have the opportunity to discuss Wanda's experience of going global at today's open lecture at Oxford University. Due to time constraints, I will make a brief speech. The remaining time will be reserved for your questions. The title of my speech is 'Going Global – The Wanda Way'. I will touch upon four main points.

1. WHY GO GLOBAL?

The first reason is to expand the size of our enterprise. To expand in certain industries, we must invest internationally. This is especially true in the entertainment or the sport industries. The international market is more developed than the Chinese market, which is an important reason for Wanda to go global.

The second reason is to become a global enterprise. In 2015, a resignation letter submitted by a professor made a sensation across China. It said: "The world is so large, I would like to see it." Let me borrow this idea to explain Wanda's reason for going global: "The world is so big, I would like to make use of it."

There were always four words at the core of Wanda's corporate culture. In 1988, when Wanda was established, I chose the following motto to be at the heart of Wanda's corporate culture: 'Be honest, be smart'. In those days, China was just going through the initial phase of economic reforms. There were many frauds among those who ventured into business. We emphasized integrity, advocating for people to 'be honest'. The second part of our motto, however, was 'be smart'. If you get cheated once, it is not your fault, but if you get cheated a second time, then it is your own fault. After some time, when the company had amassed some wealth, we changed our motto to: 'Creating wealth, benefiting society'. We advocated for everyone to take part in generating wealth while not forgetting our duty to society. In 2014, Wanda made a comprehensive improvement to its corporate culture. Our new motto appropriately expressed the company's goal, developmental policy and operational principles. It went: 'International Wanda, Centennial Business'. We were very clear what we meant by 'centennial business' – we wanted a long-lasting company. As for the meaning of "International Wanda", we were then not quite sure yet. Wanda's globalization did not set in as a direct result of the new motto. It was not until 2012 that Wanda actually started going global, but clearly the intention was there long before that.

Speaking of Wanda going global, there is another anecdote that comes to mind. It's as if Wanda were fated to become a global corporation. Originally, Wanda Group had a different name: it was called Xigang Residential Development Company. It specialized in real estate. When Wanda became a joint-stock company in 1992, we thought that this name was too tacky and decided to change it. We called for proposals for a new name and offered ¥2,000 as the reward for the winner. Around 200 people submitted proposals. We selected around ten or so from these and invited each author to introduce their logo and their suggestion for a new name for the enterprise. In the end we selected the third or fourth proposal. And this is what Wanda's logo still looks like today. The logo is dark blue with the letter W representing the shape of waves and the letter D mimicking the shape of a sailing boat. Why use blue? It is because Wanda originated from a coastal city. The two letters are enclosed within a circle, which, according to the author, signified

Wanda going global. We liked the meaning behind the logo, so we decided to adopt it. In those days, Wanda was not even a nationwide enterprise, let alone global. You can see, however, that the intention has always existed. Without having this goal and intention, we would not have got to where we are now.

The third reason for going global was to mitigate operating risks. There is a saying that goes: "Don't put all your eggs in one basket." Expanding into new markets reduces operating risks. No matter how well a country's economy is doing, there are bound to be periods of economic downturn. The likelihood of periods of economic adjustment occurring concurrently around the whole world is, however, significantly lower. The Chinese government also encourages Chinese enterprises to allocate resources around the world in order to make use of the world market. Therefore, from the point of view of mitigating operating risks, it makes sense for us to go global.

2. GLOBALIZATION STRATEGY

EMPHASIS ON MERGERS AND ACQUISITIONS

Wanda's overseas activities primarily focus on mergers and acquisitions (M&A), which are supplemented by investment. What is the reason for that? It is because since the Industrial Revolution in Britain, the world market, especially the principal sectors within it, have already been saturated by companies that entered the market first. Look at the finance industry as an example. Although I cannot say that entering the industry without M&A is absolutely impossible, it is nigh on impossible. Wanda has now turned its attention to the sports industry. The majority of proprietary and broadcasting rights for international sporting events have been taken by established family-owned companies or multinationals. The only way to enter the industry is through acquisition. A reporter once claimed in the Chinese media that "All Wanda does is buy, buy and buy." I asked him, "If we don't, what other options do we have?"

INTERCONNECTIONS

Some hold the view that Chinese enterprises never buy what is right; instead, they buy what is expensive. Wanda's key principle in going global is to buy what is right. What do I mean by that?

We evaluate two criteria. The first is that our acquisitions must be related to the industries in which Wanda already operates. On our road to globalization, the industries we entered into on a global scale are those that we were already involved in domestically. Be it real estate, culture, sports or travel, these are all fields in which we are currently involved. The advantage of that is that we already possess the right industry knowledge and the right people. We have an understanding of how things work in each particular industry.

Our second criterion, for both cross-border M&A and overseas investment projects, is that Wanda requires these businesses to be transplantable to China. Let me give you a sports enterprise M&A as an example. In 2015, Wanda acquired the world's largest triathlon company – the World Triathlon Corporation (WTC). Within half a year of the acquisition, we were able to secure triathlon events in the Chinese cities of Xiamen and Hefei. Prior to this, triathlon was not widely known in China. Only after we ran a series of promotions did the public learn exactly what triathlon was about. Currently, the number of triathletes in China is still pitifully low: out of a population larger than 1.3 billion, there are just over 200 people who practise the sport. If we promote this sport in China, we can get the number of participants up to at least several hundred thousand. There is huge potential for development in China, as people are starting to be more health-aware. Running is also becoming increasingly popular. In other countries around the world, it is extremely difficult for the WTC to grow at any decent pace. Usually, a growth rate of less than 10% is already considered an achievement. In China, however, the potential for fast growth is immense.

LOCAL TALENT

On our way to globalization, Wanda puts an emphasis on making use of local talent. Back in 2012, for example, Wanda bought AMC Theatres. The company is a cinema chain operator and the US government placed certain restrictions on the M&A of such enterprises. I went to see the US ambassador to China, Gary Locke, to ask him to write a letter recommending Wanda to the US government. His first question was whether Wanda was planning to export a large number of Chinese films to the US once it had bought AMC. I replied that that was unlikely. Even if that had been my intention, it was dependent on whether there was demand for Chinese films. If the audience did not like Chinese films, they would be sure to vote with their feet. He then asked whether Wanda was planning to fill management positions with Chinese employees. I told him that

that was not going to happen, since if management leaves as a result of an acquisition, that is an indication that the acquisition has failed. Mr Locke seemed satisfied and agreed to write a letter of recommendation for Wanda. Mr Locke's recommendation, along with other contributing factors, in the end resulted in Wanda's acquisition of AMC Theatres gaining US government approval.

Once the acquisition of AMC Theatres was accomplished, Wanda only stationed a liaison officer at the company. Wanda's acquisition of AMC raises a question. Formerly, the shareholders of AMC Theatres consisted solely of multinational enterprises. If the company was faring badly under their management, why should it be any different with Wanda in charge? Wanda came to the conclusion that the best way of handling the management of M&A was to retain the existing board of managers and motivate them to work better. Wanda's acquisition of AMC Theatres had already been turned into a case study by Harvard Business School. The professor who wrote the case study visited our offices for research purposes. He made two very classic points: on the one hand, nothing had changed – it was still the same AMC Theatres cinema chain. The name remained the same, the original management team was still in place and the location did not change. On the other hand, upon closer observation, everything had changed: the company had undergone a profound transformation. The professor's observations were spot-on.

I often say that in the past, Chinese enterprises modelled their management style on the West. We do, however, possess an advantage when it comes to applying the theories. At its most fundamental level, management is equivalent to designing an overarching system. Stimulating employees' initiative lies at the heart of the system. The aim of the system is not to impose unnecessary restrictions on the actions of the management team. The prerequisite for this kind of management was that Wanda became the majority shareholder of AMC Theatres. Prior to our acquisition, AMC Theatres was owned equally by well-known giants such as Morgan Stanley, Carlyle and Blackstone. The crucial difference was that each of these companies had a more or less equal share; there was no one company that was in charge. Wanda put an end to that. At the time when we acquired AMC Theatres, the world was still grappling with the after-effects of the global financial crisis. Jobs were nowhere near as stable as they are today. We signed a five-year work contract with the senior management team at AMC and decided that any profits over the designated targets would be shared 1:9 between the management team and Wanda. It worked wonders in stimulating the team's motivation. The company had undergone rapid transformation within a year, and the year after that it went public. This made me realize that no matter where in the world you made acquisitions, you had to try to retain the original management team, make use of and find ways to motivate the existing employees. It would be a mistake to send Chinese teams wherever you expand.

3. INTERNATIONAL DEVELOPMENT

Wanda has now become a representative of global Chinese enterprises. This is especially true among privately owned enterprises. Since 2012, within just over three years, Wanda has made investments in more than ten countries around the world. In total, the value of Wanda's investments has exceeded US$15 billion, of which US$10 billion was in the US alone; thus we enjoy great popularity in the US. When Wanda acquired AMC Theatres in 2012, I promised that within the next ten years, Wanda would invest a minimum of US$10 billion in the US. The next day, a US media company published an article titled, "We hope you honour your promise, Mr Wang." Three years later, in 2015, Wanda had already reached the investment target of US$10 billion. I asked my assistant to invite them to write a follow-up article titled, "Mr Wang fulfilled his promise – ahead of time."

Wanda invested £1.2 billion in the United Kingdom, creating 2,600 jobs. Yesterday, at the global launch of the English edition of *The Wanda Way*, we also discussed a big investment project with the British government, which we hope to launch at the earliest opportunity.

Although we have only recently set out on the road to globalization, we have been advancing smoothly and steadily, taking giant steps. Looking at Wanda's transnational expansion from a dialectical point of view, however, the fact that we have not yet failed only means that we are that much closer to failure. Wanda does not rule out the possibility of stumbling during the next phase of going global. We are guided by the principle that as long as we do not encounter a major setback, we will carry on doing what we are doing. In truth, now that we have taken the first step, going global no longer seems so daunting.

4. THE OBJECTIVES OF GOING GLOBAL

Firstly, we want to see a significant increase in revenue from overseas holdings. Last year, Wanda proposed strategic goals for the next five years, namely to achieve the

'2211' target by 2020. The number '2211' refers to having more than US$200 billion in assets, a market value of over US$200 billion, revenues of more than US$100 billion and profits of more than US$10 billion. Of this, 30% of revenues should come from overseas. One of the key indicators as to whether or not an enterprise is transnational is whether or not overseas revenues constitute over 30% of total revenues. There are two types of enterprises that encompass international business. The first is constituted by companies that produce domestically and sell globally; in this case, it is only the product that is transnational. The other type refers to companies that have investments in one or two countries overseas, but with such investments only forming a small proportion of the company's business. From the perspective of management style, HR structure and corporate culture, such enterprises cannot be considered multinational. In order to become a true multinational enterprise, a company must not only be large – with a minimum value in assets of tens of billions of US dollars – it must also generate at least 30% of revenues from abroad. This year, Wanda's overseas revenues are expected to add up to about US$10 billion, which means we still have a long way to go and a lot of work ahead of us if we want to reach our targets by 2020.

Secondly, we want to become a leading global enterprise. Wanda not only aims to become a first-class enterprise. Importantly, we want to become a first-class 'global' enterprise. If we can achieve our '2211' target, we are sure to rank among the world's top companies. This target is what drives our company and what motivates me personally to keep up the hard work. Some describe me as China's most successful entrepreneur. Many have asked how I managed to succeed. I list many reasons, but the key to my success lies in hard work. Hard work pays off. If you do not put the effort in, you have no chance of turning your vision into reality. It is because Wanda has a long-term vision that we are able to retain rapid growth. In 2015, revenue, assets and profits grew by 20% compared to 2014. Most people are awed by our speed of growth. But for Wanda, this was the first year in a long time when our annual growth rate fell below 30%. Up until now, we had managed to grow by more than 30% each year. Our growth rate has decreased slightly as a result of major restructuring of the global economy as well as a slowing Chinese economy. Yet we are still managing to retain a comparatively fast growth rate, which serves to prove that Wanda will ultimately become a leading global enterprise.

Thank you!

QUESTIONS AND ANSWERS

Host: A multinational firm needs connectivity, but also autonomy for local managers. Is there a tension between trying to pull together connectivity within Wanda companies while also giving them autonomy?

Wang Jianlin: We now have a lot of senior employees in Wanda that we have trained over their many years with the company. Now that we have entered new industries and the company is becoming multinational, lack of English knowledge is proving to be a problem. Industries like tourism, sport and entertainment all require frequent contact with foreigners. Although we have a lot of good people, they cannot be put to good use because of their inadequacy in the English language.

At the moment, there are two types of people that we look for. First, Chinese people with good English are at an advantage. Second, we look for foreigners who can speak Chinese. There are many foreigners in China, and some speak even better Chinese than the average Chinese person. I say that there is no standard answer for how an enterprise should be managed. In my opinion, one always has to rely on oneself to come up with a solution. That's as much as I have to say about this.

Host: Many of the Chinese enterprises that attempt to go global are state-owned enterprises, yet they have been unsuccessful so far. The following question is from James Kynge of the *Financial Times*: Is part of the reason why these enterprises have encountered problems in overseas investments the fact that they are not commercially motivated?

Wang Jianlin: First let me make it clear that there are private enterprises that have successfully become global companies, but there are also state-owned enterprises that have managed to make a success of globalization. Overall, however, private enterprises do tend to do better than state-owned enterprises. I believe that this is because the managers of private enterprises stay in their posts longer. It is extremely difficult for the managers of state-owned enterprises to set long-term goals, as they have two or three years in their posts before they are replaced. I see this as a problem. Apart from the difference in the length of office, the organizational structure of state-owned enterprises does not favour internationalization. The approval processes within these enterprises are too lengthy.

Wanda is building one of the tallest buildings on the Thames riverbank in London. It will house one of

London's most luxurious hotels. It can be said that we basically got the hotel for this project for free. Wanda's overseas development manager just happened to be on a business trip to London, when he by chance discovered that a bank was planning to put this unprofitable asset up for auction. The bank offered the hotel to Wanda, under the condition that we would pay up within a week – otherwise it was going to be auctioned. The public auction price was bound to shoot up. The development manager gave me a call and I thought he must have misheard. He said that they were asking for £900 per square metre. Surely he must have misheard! I asked him to check with the bank again. With my many years' experience in real estate, asking for £9,000 per square metre would make more sense. The development manager got back to me, having checked the price. It was indeed £900 per square metre. I told him to sign the contract immediately. We made a down payment within three days. If Wanda had been a state-owned company, we would never have been able to make such a quick decision.

Host: Only last month you acquired Legendary Pictures. When you mentioned Wanda's competitive advantage in real estate, you emphasized the executive force. You yourself are someone who excels at bringing results. My question is, do you also put a strong emphasis on execution in the cultural industry?

Wang Jianlin: Bringing results is not only important in real estate. No matter what industry you are in, you have to perform. I remember that Jack Welch, a famous management guru and the former CEO of General Electric, once said that execution is the key to a company's success. In enterprise management, one can implement countless strategies to drive results, but according to Welch all it boils down to in the end is the power of execution. I could not agree more with this view. This is why we have annual plans at the start of each year for all our industries, ranging from film to sport and entertainment. Our plans need to be detailed. We have weekly plans for capital allocation, cash flows and so on. At Wanda, we use a modular system to work out plans for each module of work. Each module is split into a number of individual tasks. If a task along the way is not completed, the system marks it with a yellow light. If two yellow lights come on at once, the system marks the whole module in red. At this stage, we follow up with appropriate punishments. There are those who maintain that people who work in the cultural industry should wear slippers and T-shirts to work; in particular, wearing suits and ties does not go well with the entertainment industry. There is a popular saying in China that goes, "I don't believe that great ideas can be confined by suits." Great ideas are born in the brain; they have nothing to do with suits and ties!

I put great emphasis on execution, which is why Wanda has created a business model that is unique around the world. Each year we open dozens of large-scale commercial centres, 20 or so hotels and a number of other projects in the entertainment and tourist industries. We set deadlines for opening dates and we stick to them. It may sound simple, but in fact it is no easy feat. My understanding of the executive force is that it is the key competitive advantage of any enterprise in any sector. People who believe that there is no need to emphasize execution in the entertainment or internet industries have an incomplete understanding of the basics of management.

Audience member: I was very impressed with your policy of offering incentives of 10% of the profits to your managers. I own five hotels in the UK, but I can't afford to give 10% of the profits to my managers. How do you manage your incentives in the hotel trade?

Wang Jianlin: How many hotels does Wanda own? In China, we operate almost 100 five-star hotels. We now have seven hotels abroad. There are two types of hotels that we manage in China. The first type is made up of hotels that are directly operated by Wanda. These are managed by Wanda's own hotel management company. About one third of our hotels are managed on our behalf. There are about 20 of these hotels which are managed by the global hotel management companies that we are all familiar with.

In a favourable economic environment, it is hard to see the difference in management between the two types. After President Xi Jinping's Eight-Point Regulation in 2012, however, the difference between the two types became apparent. The hotels that were managed by external companies all failed to complete their operating targets. Those managed by Wanda, however, all succeeded in fulfilling their targets. The key to our success was the Wanda modular work plan system. Within this system, reports on revenues and costs are submitted daily. We require each of our companies to make daily reports so that each day we know exactly how we are doing in terms of revenue, costs and profits. If after half a year you suddenly realize that you are not on track to fulfil your target, it is normally too late. We employ the same method in hotel management. We make sure that we set daily and weekly targets, so that we stay on track. If we solely relied on material incentives, then where would the incentives come from if we hadn't met our profit targets in the first place? In my opinion hotel management is no different from management in other industries. Hotel management might be slightly harder as we are dealing with the top end of luxury brands. It incorporates a greater variety of services including entertainment, catering and accommodation, but in practice, the management strategy is the same. This is how I would describe Wanda's hotel management approach.

Audience member: I work for a British corporation. During the last couple of years Wanda has been making rapid progress in overseas mergers and acquisitions. Last autumn, during President Xi's visit to Britain, the UK and China welcomed a 'golden age' of Sino-British relations. Has Wanda considered the possibility of establishing strategic cooperation with top-class British businesses that would allow Wanda to enter other newly developing markets around the world, on top of the Chinese and British markets?

Wang Jianlin: Well, thank you for the suggestion. My priority is to first assure Wanda's own successful globalization. Last year I met with the UK Trade Department in order to invite British businesses willing to develop the Chinese market to come to China. Wanda can provide the developmental platform for such businesses. We are a platform provider. Wanda Plazas and Wanda Holiday Resorts are not operated by Wanda. We just manage these platforms and only operate a small section ourselves. If businesses are willing to come to China, I am willing to provide the developmental platform, be it in the textile industry, catering, cosmetics or whatever.

I am currently involved in two activities. Firstly, I make investments and secondly, I take British businesses to

China. Now, your suggestion that we establish cooperation with British businesses to open up the world market is indeed a mighty vision. I hope that in the future I might be able to realize your goal.

Audience member: What is the driving force behind your hard work? Is it a personal ideal, wealth or a sense of social responsibility?

Wang Jianlin: It changed with time. In the initial stages, my motivation for keeping going was to live a better life. I originally worked for the government. When I switched to doing business, my objective was very simple: I wanted to have a better life. When I started the business, my employees told me that once we reached ¥100 million we could retire. In those days, profit of even tens of thousands was rarely seen, let alone 100 million. I had not thought that we would reach this goal so quickly. I discovered that we set our goal too low, so I set us a new goal: to grow the company and become a well-known enterprise. Achieving such a goal would be a worthy feat.

I think that the most important step for Wanda was in 1993, when it expanded from Dalian and turned from a local business into a nationwide one. We must not forget that expanding across China is the equivalent of expanding across twice the size of Europe. China covers an area twice as big as Europe, and China's population is also twice that of Europe. During Wanda's second developmental stage, my objective was to turn Wanda into a well-known enterprise.

Recently, I have been driven by yet another goal. My vision became even greater. I want to make the Wanda brand globally recognized. I want Wanda to become a top-class enterprise. I cannot tell you the exact figures, but we have internally set the target to be ranked among world's most successful companies by 2020. We have not reached this target yet. Perhaps, if we reach this target in 2020, 2019 or maybe even 2018, I might retire. Or maybe I might set myself another target.

Several years ago, when the company earned revenues of around ¥10 billion, I told my senior managers that when we got to 100 billion I would definitely retire. Thanks to the rapid development of the Chinese economy, a company can just ride on the wave of economic development and grow by 8% or 9% each year without even trying too hard. If you put some effort in, you can even grow by around 20% annually. Within five or six years, we had reached our target. My employees asked me, "Are you retiring?" It still seemed a bit too early for me to retire. Now the target we have set for ourselves is to become a leading global enterprise. By 2020, we want to rank among the top global enterprises. I might not retire even then. I might stop working day by day the way it is now, or I might do something else entirely.

I set targets for different stages of development. During the course of our life, we have different targets that are realistic for each stage of our life. It is good practice to constantly adjust one's goals, as only then can they be achieved. Many years ago I set up a personal entrepreneurial fund to support young entrepreneurs. Three years ago, Wanda set up its own entrepreneurial fund. Each year we devote ¥50 million to the fund. We are doing quite well, with a success rate of 95% or more consecutively for the past several years. Of course, we have a strategy. Each entrepreneur is allocated two supervisors. There was one young entrepreneur who came to see me several times. I told him: "We have an application process that has several stages to it, but since you have made the effort to see me, I will make an exception. You don't need to apply. I will write you a letter of recommendation and directly give you several million yuan to get you started." Guess what the man told me? He said, "How could several million be enough?" I asked him how much he wanted. He replied, "At the very least, several hundred million." I said, "Did you know that several hundred million is not called starting a new business! That is called succeeding in running a business."

My point is that you asked a very good question. People should set realistic goals during their lives – goals that are achievable and that can be adjusted along the way.

Audience member: Seeing as you are so busy, I would like to ask whether you have a way of allocating time just for yourself, or whether work is everything for you.

Wang Jianlin: Work is not everything, but work is the most important thing. Even though I would like to give myself some time off, I can't! Why is that? When I want to have a rest, my underlings keep calling me all the time. I am not dealing with operations directly any more, my main duty is to meet with people. Whenever someone important comes, I have to make time for them to make the follow-up work easier for my employees. When foreign guests arrive, should I see them or not? Of course I have to see them. My main duties nowadays are limited to meeting people over lunch or dinner.

Audience member: I would like to ask you a question relating to M&A. As a result of the current unfavourable global economic environment, businesses find it difficult to make decent profits. Although this pushes their market valuations down, they may not be facing bright developmental

prospects. From the point of view of a publicly listed company, launching acquisitions of such companies will undoubtedly present a financial burden during the initial stages after the acquisition. How does Wanda balance cheap valuations with unsure business prospects?

Wang Jianlin: In fact, any point in time is suitable for doing good business. You mentioned cheap market valuations, but that would only apply from a short-term perspective, maybe looking two or three years into the future. In such a situation, you can say that something is expensive or cheap. If you, however, look at acquisitions from a long-term perspective, say ten years, then it does not matter which company is cheap. Let's assume that the current market valuation is low so you decide to make an acquisition. Is that a guarantee that in the future the market valuation is bound to increase? Not necessarily. The most important thing in M&A is what I mentioned before – choosing the correct assets and choosing the right direction. Will the acquisition result in further supporting your business? Will the acquisition expand your business? Can you use the acquisition to help you enter a new industry and expand your scope? These are the things we should consider in M&A.

As for slightly cheaper or more expensive market valuation, that is for investors to decide, not for entrepreneurs.

Audience member: A lot of people are interested in the strategy for Wanda in the UK. What is the strategy in the country and where do you think the good investments are in the UK? And if the UK leaves the EU, will it be less attractive as an investment?

Wang Jianlin: I will first answer the question about the EU. I do not think the UK will leave the EU. My opinion is based on inferences but I might be wrong. First, from a historical point of view, the UK has never been separate from Europe. Secondly, the UK would struggle to manage alone in today's globalized economy. There is no guarantee that if the UK left the EU, it would be in a stronger position. There is no way of saying whether it would be a better or worse position. And finally, leaving the EU would be easy, but trying to get back in would be hard. Without doubt, there would be more disadvantages than advantages for the UK if it left the EU. That is what I think, but I am not a politician.

As for Wanda's standing in the UK, I believe that the UK and the US are the two countries of greatest interest to Wanda. Why did I invest US$10 million in the US? Because the country is big and its population is large as well. The simple logic is that Wanda entered because of the attractive market potential. Although the UK's population and market are comparatively smaller, the UK ranks first in the world in terms of market freedom. The US is nicknamed the 'Land of the Free', yet companies need to get approval for their investments from the Department of Commerce as well as from the Committee on Foreign Investment. If you are caught doing business without approval, your enterprise can be banned from operating on US soil any time within 50 years of the breach. Other countries have even more rules. The UK is the most liberal; its laws and other aspects are also well suited for investment. The UK also boasts an impressive service industry. Wanda is very keen to turn the UK into the centre for its European investments.

I mentioned that we were in the course of discussing a multi-billion-euro project with the British Minister of State for Trade. Once this project is in place, we might consider locating our headquarters for the whole of Europe in the

UK. Once the London hotel starts operating, it will create 3,000 new jobs. We are also currently in the process of discussing an integrated project within the entertainment sector that would create 10,000 new jobs. I think that this is sufficient to show the level of importance we attach to the UK. Besides, my son also studied in the UK.

Audience member: There is a lot of worry about China right now. What do you think are the biggest risks facing China and what do you think are the reforms that are needed to keep the economy going forward?
Wang Jianlin: The greatest challenge China is facing today is the restructuring of its economy. The Chinese economy relies on three pillars. In the past, investment took up the largest proportion, followed by exports and then finally consumption. Export is not going as smoothly as it used to in the past. This is because the global economy, including the European economy, has still not recovered from the financial crisis. Exports are therefore lagging behind. As for investments, all that could be invested in pretty much has been. There are not many opportunities for new investments with high rates of return.

Now the economy must undergo a process of restructuring, be it active or passive. During this process, economic development is going to slow down. If it comes to a major slowdown, we might see a rise in unemployment. So the greatest challenge for the Chinese economy is industrial restructuring. There must be a period of restructuring whether we like it or not. There is no way to avoid it. If the restructuring comes in a passive form, it will be a lot harder. We can now see a gradual trend that economic growth is slowing down.

The economic restructuring also presents us with opportunities. Our ancestors who invented the Chinese language were very precise in their descriptions. The term for 'crisis' in the Chinese language consists of two characters, one meaning 'danger' and the other 'opportunity'. Therefore, crisis does not necessarily mean danger; it also provides us with opportunities. This stems from Laozi's dialectical thought. The word for crisis was well chosen.

Let me give you an example. The manufacturing sector and the export sector are struggling, but at the same time the service, entertainment and tourist sectors are all experiencing rapid growth. Last year, outbound tourism in China grew by 20%. Chinese tourists spent trillions of yuan overseas, maybe even more. So, the answer to the question of how to restructure the Chinese economy is to identify the right direction for development and target domestic demand. Ample opportunities exist, especially in the domestic sector, with demand for entertainment, sports and travel.

Audience member: Over the last 30 years, a lot of the innovation in China has come from local officials who are willing to try new things. The anti-corruption drive caused many local officials to be afraid of innovating. Do we not have need of bold reform to move society forward?

Wang Jianlin: These two aspects are not related. Actually, I believe that not fighting corruption would pose an even bigger problem. Currently, the Chinese economy is experiencing a slowdown, or in some places, local officials are not doing as much as they should. The root of the problem is that the administrative system itself is flawed. Further work needs to be put into exploring ways of providing encouraging incentives while at the same time strengthening anti-corruption measures. It would be wrong to say, however, that because of the anti-corruption drive local officials are not doing their work. At least from the perspective of people involved in the business sector, we think that things have changed for the better. This is especially true for private businesses. Perhaps state-owned enterprises do not feel the same way, but for us privately owned companies, the anti-corruption policies have spared us a lot of hassle and saved us a lot of money.

Student: Thank you for your speech today. I really think that hearing you speak is better than studying for ten years. I originally meant to ask some questions relating to macroeconomy, but they have already been answered. I believe my question will be of interest to many people in the audience here today. You mentioned that Wanda employs 18,000 people in the US and 2,600 in the UK. As you said, you are planning to launch a project in the UK that will create 10,000 new jobs. How can we be of use to Wanda? As ethnic Chinese students who can speak fluent English, it would be a great honour for us to contribute to a leading Chinese global enterprise like Wanda.

Wang Jianlin: Would you like to work in China or in the UK?

Student: I would prefer the UK.

Wang Jianlin: As I said, we are currently working out whether or not this major project can make its way to the UK. We proposed the project over two years ago, but for a number of reasons, it has not gone through. Now the UK is lagging behind other destinations. This week, I am heading to another country for two days to launch a major project there. It is a shame that it was not possible for the UK to be the first choice of destination for this project. Originally the UK was under consideration. Well, even though the project in the UK might not be the first of its kind, we will make it the best of its kind. It might be the second or third such project, but when it is finalized, it will create at least 10,000 new jobs. Since you speak such good English, you would definitely be a priority for us. Don't think I am fooling with you – we are being broadcast live! Just say that you asked a question at the Oxford University open lecture and I will take you on.

Student: Thank you! I will makebe sure to remember that.
Wang Jianlin: Let me add to that. All Oxford graduates will be first in line to work at Wanda.

Student: Let me thank Chairman Wang on behalf of all us!
Audience member: I am from London Business School. The 1980s and 1990s in China produced many successful entrepreneurs. They became heroes of private Chinese enterprises. Starting in 2012, however, the Chinese economy encountered a downturn. Today's environment is different from the one in which you started. What advice and guidance would you have for young entrepreneurs today?
Wang Jianlin: Actually, the environment today is better suited for start-ups than back then. When I started my company, I had a registered capital of ¥500,000, which I borrowed. Guess the interest rate on the loan? 25% annual interest, and the principal had to be returned within five years. Nowadays there are many start-ups. I personally support

100 entrepreneurial projects each year. There are many who give support to young entrepreneurs. The key is getting access to funds. The most important part is preparing a business plan capable of attracting start-up capital. Simply speaking, your plan must be feasible. Don't emphasize the bad points. You must learn to say the right things to make people believe that you are reliable. Some young start-up entrepreneurs aim too high. They say they want to be an industry or world leader, but as soon as people hear that, they do not dare to invest in you. Be realistic in what you can achieve. You don't necessarily need to be involved in technology. Traditional industries hold as many opportunities as ever. The reason they are called traditional industries is that they are long-lasting and resilient. Innovative industries have the advantage of high profits and fast increases in value, but by the same logic they die just as quickly.

My advice to you is to choose your partners well or to seek the guidance of a trained supervisor. Wanda has entrepreneurial guides for graduates. I don't know what your name is, but if you are interested in applying, we have an official application process. Everyone who asked questions today has a book signed by me. Since *you* asked today, you are definitely going to be top of my list.